Also by Don Cupitt and published by SCM Press

Christ and the Hiddenness of God
Creation out of Nothing
Crisis of Moral Authority
The Leap of Reason
Life Lines
The Long-Legged Fly
The New Christian Ethics
Only Human
Radicals and the Future of the Church
Taking Leave of God
The World to Come
What is a Story?

Don Cupitt

THE TIME BEING

SCM Press

British Library Cataloguing-in-Publication Data

Cupitt, Don
Time Being
I. Title
230
ISBN 0–334–02522–2

A catalogue record for this book is available
from the British Library

First British edition published 1992
by SCM Press Ltd
26–30 Tottenham Road, London N1 4BZ

Typeset by Intype, London
Printed in Great Britain by
Mackays of Chatham, Kent

for Caroline

Contents

Preface

Dōgen, who might be called the Japanese Meister Eckhart, has a good saying about the act of reading the *Lotus Sutra*. This discourse by the Buddha would have been known to him in the form of a little stack of oblong palm-leaves, on which the text was painted. During the reading they are turned like the pages of a Western book. Dōgen says: 'If the mind is deluded, the *Lotus Sutra* turns us; if the mind is enlightened, we turn it; and if we transcend illusion and enlightenment, the *Lotus Sutra* turns the *Lotus Sutra*.'[1]

To attain the very highest degree of freedom we must transcend all duality. The duality between subject and object goes, and the self therefore disappears. In addition, the duality between nirvana and the horizontal flow of time from moment to moment *also* goes. 'Impermanence is Buddha-nature': Dōgen teaches a mysticism of transience. The purely contingent now of being-time, the time of our life, is in effect equated by him with the Eternal Now that in Western thought is ascribed to God alone.

Dōgen is a beautiful thinker, but his message doesn't come very easily to us in the West. We have been accustomed to a strong conception of the human self, especially in religion, and also to a strong conception of eternity. We have always tended to disparage the transient and the insubstantial as being unsatisfying to the soul. An immortal substance itself, the soul wants to be nourished with immortal food, nothing less.

Today, however, our conception of the human subject is becoming very much weaker. The self has been brought down into culture and the flow of historical time. Everything it is can be described in terms of its cultural setting, its relationships, its circumstances, its life and its activities. That is, it is composed entirely of what is relative and transient. It has come down in the world. It has lost its old metaphysical substantiality.

We are thus getting ourselves into a rather Buddhist cultural condition. It might be called 'a post-Buddhism of the sign'. Life has become aestheticized: everything is turning into a flux of transient cultural products – feelings, meanings, theories, goods, symbols, fashions, recordings, artworks, images and words. This makes us very uneasy. Coming out of a Christian background, we expect there to be a solid and intelligible order of things around us. That after all is what we suppose our forebears to have had, so we feel that we are entitled to more of the same. We find ourselves asking: 'Look, how can there be religion without a strong religious subject? How can we hope to affirm the possibility of human freedom and joy and creativity in the face of the disappearance of the human subject? And if indeed everything is transient, how can there be a *religion* of pure contingency? Surely one cannot simply equate God, or the Buddha-nature, or whatever it be called, with the flux of coming-to-be and passing away? Surely religion has got to be about what is real and undying?'

When we meet these questions we Westerners tend to drop into our traditional dualistic vocabulary. We imagine ourselves as being able to say Yes to the fleeting only in so far as we can learn to perceive it as veiling an enduring Reality that underlies it. At least since the time of Plato, we have made the transient bearable by jumping immediately to its polar opposite. The changing is claimed somehow to presuppose the unchanging, the relative reminds us of the Absolute, death becomes 'eternity' – and so on.

These manoeuvres are currently ceasing to work, mainly because we now recognize that they are after all only linguistic customs, consolatory gestures prescribed by our culture. Their status is about the same as that of the proverbs which assure us that the darkest cloud has a silver lining and it is best always to look on the bright side. So the question now becomes one of whether we can say a full religious Yes to the fleeting as such, in the sober recognition that it is all there is. We teeter all the time on the brink of nothingness, and however careful we are to keep our balance, we will in due course drop off. Can we therefore make religion, real religion, out of our new-found utter insecurity, secondariness and transience?

For us, with our background in Christianity and Greek philosophy, these are difficult questions. But Japan has some experience in this area, which is perhaps one reason why it is doing so well nowadays. The large collection of Japanese prints in Claude Monet's house at Giverny suggests an affinity between Japanese Buddhism and what the Impressionists were trying to achieve. A mysticism of the insubstantial, of the senses and of the fleeting moment. Northern or Mahayana Buddhism was non-realist from very early times. As early as Nagarjuna it was being taught that the blissful state of *nirvana* and the cycles of birth and death, *samsara*, are not polar opposites.[2] Rather, the truly enlightened person comes to see them as identical. Eternal happiness is not located in another world distinct from the world of time and the senses, but rather is a way of saying Yes to this world.

It ought to be possible to develop a similar line of thought within our Western tradition, even though there are obvious difficulties. It is true that we have tended to regard the religious object as eternal and absolute Reality, and to associate salvation with complete security. By the same token, although we have always permitted our poets to celebrate sensuous transient beauty, we have carefully added the proviso that the celebration needs to take the form of a pagan lament over something profane that is doomed soon to pass away. The monks of the Western Middle Ages, as Umberto Eco has emphasized, had an acute sense of earthly beauty – but extolled it only in order to make the point that it was merely outward and perishing.[3] We should therefore turn away from it, and attend to the eternal and imperishable beauty of God and of divine things. So in our dominant tradition, in the religious orders and in the language of prayer, true religion has always portrayed itself as concerned only with eternal and enduring things. It has opposed itself to and called pagan everything that is 'merely' outward, of this world, relative and transient. The long-term outcome, now that the outward, temporal, transient and relative has become all there is, is that many people feel that the Christian tradition has come to an end, and nothing is left to us except the lyrical melancholy paganism of the poets.[4]

I am suggesting, however, that this is to ignore Mahayana Buddhism. It is also to ignore certain major strands within the Christian tradition. The most important is the doctrine of the incarnation, which was from the outset seen as conjoining again everything that the platonic dualisms had disjoined – the eternal and the temporal, absolute and relative, necessary and contingent and so on. This bridging of the oppositions creates a possibility of mysticism and dialectical movement within Christianity. At different stages in the unfolding of the rhetoric, divine things and human things are first to be radically contrasted with each other, and then to be equally radically conjoined and inseparably united.

Both platonism and incarnation are central to the Western tradition; and the implications of this trite observation are considerable. It means that for us, too, truth could never be wholly pinned down in bald dogmatic metaphysical assertions. Rather, truth is revealed through a series of rhetorical movements which act first to devalue the transient, and then to revalue it. That's all we mean by truth: a world marked out, ordered, valued and revalued in language. At different stages in the argument we humans are first worthless and damnable, and then become 'other Christs', sons and daughters of God. Life is thus made worth living. What else is all talk in aid of? And as truth thus becomes thoroughly dialectical, we find ourselves drawing closer to the old Buddhist philosophers after all.

So in the present text I'm trying to make afresh a series of rather traditional gestures. I'm trying to find ways of saying what our condition now is, what is the nature of our discontent, and what the cure. An old enquiry, which keeps on needing to be renewed. Because of the course that events have taken we have much to learn from the Buddhist tradition, especially the early Indian

Madhyamika and Japanese Zen. But our own tradition, boldly handled, can also be developed to meet the new situation.

We must attend very closely to what Dōgen calls *uji*, 'being-time', and what the West calls 'the changes and chances of this mortal life'.[5] In that area we pose our questions, and in that area find our answers.

This, by the way, is the third of a little group of 'expressionist' books. The earlier ones were *Creation out of Nothing* (1990), about language, and *What is a Story?* (1991), about narrativity. Thanks again to Linda Allen for typing and to Hugh Rayment-Pickard for suggestions and corrections.

I

REDEFINITIONS

We are talking about a new beginning and about deliberately changing various meanings. Not a popular idea, because our culture, like every other, cannot help being traditionalist. It has to put up a fiction to the effect that currently established meanings are natural and original. They have come down to us, they don't change, and it is a sin even to try to change them. In relatively stable times, when meanings are evolving only slowly, many people are ready to accept this fiction. In which case they will register their repugnance at some cultural innovation or other by arguing that it falls outside existing definitions. That is not art, they will assert confidently. Even in the most advanced societies it is very common for people to object strongly to innovations simply on the ground that they are novel.

There's nothing surprising about this. A meaning is simply a tradition, an historically-evolved social custom. Any innovation that involves modifying established usages is bound to be difficult to understand and painful to adjust to. Nevertheless it can happen that in times of rapid change meanings actually need to be shifted. Old customs are simply no longer working well, and have to be modified. Innovation in such circumstances will still meet at first with all the usual reproaches. They may be violent: the impulse to cast out or burn the offending novelty can be astonishingly strong. For a while. But if the avant-garde item is pushing in the right general direction what is equally astonishing is the sheer rapidity with which it can be assimilated and become canonical.

Modern painting provides the most familiar examples. In the later nineteenth century a whole long-established ideology of

6

painting was crumbling. A new commercial and industrial civilization needed a new kind of art. Old ideas about representation,
about Nature and about Beauty were losing their grip. Painters
wanted to break away from the controlling authorities which had
traditionally directed their work – the aristocracy, the church and
the academies. The boundaries of what was possible in art were
being shifted by such factors as a better knowledge of non-
European cultures, and the camera. For all sorts of reasons it was
necessary to produce works of art that fell outside existing
definitions – with results that everybody knows.

Not surprisingly, the cleverest and most self-confident artists
began in due course to cock a snook at the public. Their work
anticipates and laughs at the knee-jerk hostility it knows it will
encounter. Pablo Picasso mounted a cycle saddle on a stand with
a pair of handlebars above it, and called the result *Bull's Head*.
Like many other Picasso sculptures, the work is still delightful
because it is so impishly provocative. A much higher degree
of self-reflexivity and compression was achieved by Marcel
Duchamp when he exhibited a white porcelain men's urinal,
titling it *Fountain*. The work is the artist's response to its own
critical reception. Of course, says Duchamp, you the public
invariably want to piss on anything new in art, so here is a
work of art expressly designed to accommodate the response
it is sure to provoke. Now go ahead, if you dare.

Another example, also very highly self-reflexive: Andy Warhol,
in 1964, wanted to say something about the supremacy in the
modern world of the consumer product. Wrapped up in its brand
image, its packaging, its design and so forth, the consumer product
has become super-aestheticized. Under free-market capitalism the
product cannot have got where it is without being unbeatably
competitive. It is as seductive, memorable, easy on the eye and
user-friendly as millions of dollars of investment can make it. No
wonder it rules the world, and no wonder art cannot compete
with it. It has superseded the old Art-type art. So Warhol put a
cardboard *Brillo Box* on display at the Stable Gallery, New York.[1]

In each case the question arises, Is it art? In each case the work itself sets out to prompt that question, art having now become self-conscious. In each case the work is art all right, for it has become part of the canonical history of twentieth-century art, and it makes art-sense when talked about. And in each case, too, the work is anti-realist in my sense: it is fully twentieth-century, definition-questioning, self-reflexive, transgressive. It is anti-realist because it declines to conform to established genres and expectations ('reality', please note, is nothing but such conformity) and its artistic point is the particular manner in which it deviates, and so disturbs its audience. It is not asking to be accepted as orthodox. It is not trying to confirm existing ways of thinking. Don't complain that it is like a slap in the face, because it is intended to be like a slap in the face – but from a Zen abbot.

It has often been said that we need changes in philosophy and religion comparable with what has happened in painting. We need to turn reflexively back and criticize the subject itself, we need to change meanings that are no longer useful, and we need to cause a good deal of offence. In philosophy – in American neo-pragmatism and in French philosophy, for example – there is some reason to think that long-overdue changes are now at last taking place. In religious thought there has been less progress, because there hasn't been much effort. It is time to start being seriously bloody-minded.

Why? A well-known saying of Nietzsche gives a clue: I fear we'll not get rid of God, he remarks, until we can get rid of grammar. He means that theological ways of thinking are much more pervasive and harder to dispense with than people yet realize. In this context, the word 'theological' means more or less the same as the words 'metaphysical', or 'platonic'. It refers to the style of thinking which explains the manifest by unifying and grounding it in some hidden and higher-level Reality. For example, people postulate grammar as a unifying, controlling and abiding intellectual structure that underlies the surface phenomena of language. We like to see grammar as a hidden *a priori* standing behind language, very much as God stands behind the phenomena of the world: inescapable, always presupposed, and there whether people advert to it or not.

Nietzsche would certainly have regarded Noam Chomsky's theories about grammar and syntax as being highly theological in form. The surface flux of phenomena – that is, everyday talk and writing – cannot stand alone, but needs to be explained at a deeper level. And the thing that does the explaining has to have a number of the attributes of God. It must be unified, rational, law-giving, hidden, authoritative, unchanging and so forth.

Generalizing from this example, we can move on to see theological ways of thinking as being still almost ubiquitous. They are especially prominent wherever conservative educationists and academies are to be heard stressing the importance of first principles, rules, theories, rudiments, discipline, groundwork, elements and formal training.

However, most people learnt to speak and write their native language without ever articulating the rules of grammar and syntax. Most of us when learning a game find it easier to pick up the rules as we go along, and there are many cases where a developing custom or tradition generates its own deep structure as it goes. People did after all speak grammatically for millennia before there was any consciously-worked-out subject called grammar. Recently, the way we bring our language-use under rule as we go along has been successfully computer-modelled.

This indicates that the apriorism of the conservatives must be mistaken. In learning anything, you don't have to learn the formal structure first, and you don't even have to presuppose the prior existence of the formal structure. Rather, the formal structure comes to be worked out much later. It is a secondary fiction, invented by scholars. There is no need to mythicize it. Certainly it has been mythicized, historically. That is why our culture developed the standard contrasts between the *a priori* and the *a posteriori*, theory and practice, God and the world, the eternal and the temporal, noumena and phenomena, and so forth. Entrenched theological ways of thinking still in almost all quarters prompt us to distinguish between changing surface phenomena and a prior unchanging deep structure behind them. But today those ways of thinking are at last coming to an end. Old assumptions, distinctions and binary oppositions are being questioned. We are finally giving up the ancient idea that everything is two-levelled. Instead, we are developing a new style of thinking, temporal, pragmatic and horizontal. Structure of every kind is coming to be seen as improvised and emergent within the flow of practice. Formal structures (rules, meanings, standards and the like) are not laid up in heaven. They are not timeless, and they do not occupy a different level of being. We may come along later to abstract them from the flux and formalize them; but so far as their first appearance is concerned, grammar evolves immanently within the use of language, standards evolve immanently within practices and so on. Nobody preplanned the *a priori*. It just grew.

Result? The end of metaphysical theology as we've known it so far, and the purging of residually-theological ways of thinking from the culture. God's second death. That's why I'm saying that we urgently need to cause offence by changing meanings and developing new ways of thinking.

The common requirement in painting, philosophy and theology alike is that we've got to get rid of the old appearance-reality distinction, and therewith of a whole cluster of ideas about representation, knowledge and truth.[2]

The general theme is clear enough by now. The appearance-reality distinction always wants to make the world two-layered. In the foreground, immediately before us, there is the apparent: it is perhaps the sensuous image, or it is the painted representation, or it is the symbols and teachings of a religion, or it is an explanatory model or a descriptive sentence. Anyhow, the apparent foreground object is supposed to be a picture of the way things are in the real order out there on the far side of it. Condemned to secondariness, we don't see the Real directly. We see only images, models, words and the like which are supposed to represent reality to us. In which case truth is thought to consist in a certain correspondence or copying-relation between the foreground apparent object and the Original or the Real standing hidden behind it.

The relation of appearance to reality is a bit like that of messenger to master, and a bit like that of clothing to the body. The messenger who acts as an envoy or spokesman has the task of standing for or representing his master in a foreign environment. The movement of loose flowing clothes may hint at the shape of the body they conceal.

However, the apparent is always in an awkward double-bind. It is defined as being in every possible respect the polar opposite of the Real. It is merely a picture, merely a human image, merely transient and particular. As such, it is unsatisfying, and even unintelligible. It is quite inadequate to the Real beyond it. In fact, it gets about as bad a press as could be imagined. It seems totally unqualified to do the job which nevertheless is thrust upon it, of mediating to us a knowledge of the Real. So we find ourselves being told a number of different things that just don't hang together. To take a religious example, let's suppose that the apparent object is a series of sentences about God – a page of text with, perhaps, the Creed printed on it. Then we are told, first that this object before us truly represents to us the way things are in the real invisible order out there beyond the page; secondly, that this text, like all language and indeed like everything merely apparent and sensuous, is radically inadequate to the Real; and thirdly, that we can't actually check the point anyway, because nobody is ever going to walk into Heaven with a page of sentences and hold them up to see if they are the same shape as God.

The appearance-reality distinction gives rise to an intellectual nightmare of this form everywhere that its influence reaches, and especially in connection with our ideas about language, science, theory, metaphysics and religious belief. That is why we want to get shot of it. Fast. It also has pernicious moral consequences. Ever since Plato it has tended to work in favour of other-worldliness, long-termism and rationalism. It is curiously sexist. It robs of value everything close at hand, short term, particular, living, moving, sensuous and affecting.[3] Our dominant tradition has always assured us with a certain relish that all the joys and beauties of the apparent or visible world will eventually crumble to dust. Nothing in this whole world is to be loved and trusted unless it lasts for ever. Fleeting goods aren't real goods at all. So in the end nothing matters *at all* except death, things eternal, faith and the virtues. Everything else is dross.

Most of the great world religions have been other-worldly in outlook and have taken a dim view of this world. How has it come about that vigorous civilizations have been founded upon such pessimistic faiths? The answer is that religion has helped to socialize people precisely by training them to take the long view, avoid distractions and organize their whole lives towards the attainment of a single far-off goal. Just because religion so forcefully inculcates the appearance-reality distinction, it makes people into rational long-termists. Religion is thus a highly civilizing influence. It teaches us to relate ourselves to our bodies, our senses and our passions pretty much as God relates himself to the world. God's rational world-control is a model for human rational self-control. Religion makes life literally eccentric – that is, organized around a Centre outside itself – for it trains us always to regard the manifest world as subject to the control of something hidden, enduring and lawlike in its operation. Because God was the Principle of all intelligibility, theology really was the queen of the sciences, and provided as we have seen the pattern for the construction of the other branches of culture. Natural science is theological in so far as it postulates an unchanging and coherent mathematical pattern behind the changing appearances of Nature. Art (at least up to Ruskin's *Modern Painters*, volume III)[4] sought to be so faithful in its representation of Nature that it would somehow reveal in Nature the handiwork of Nature's God. Just the natural form, represented with sufficient skill and reverence, would become a refracted image of the eternal Beauty. Similarly, unchanging divine Law underlay and governed not only the natural order but also, and in different modes, the moral order, the state and the church. An analogy of Law was pictured as ordering and sustaining all things – and even today we still use the word law in a family of senses that reflects the old belief.

Nevertheless, and in spite of the admitted power of all these ideas, I am still saying that they are ugly now, they don't work, and we've got to get rid of them. We must get rid of the appearance-reality distinction and all its works, including all the theology and the long-termist religion that went with it. We've got to give up the long-faced, repressed and other-worldly religiosity that Nietzsche so rightly excoriated, and we've got to reject the repulsive idea that whatever is perishable and therefore 'corruptible' can have no intrinsic value.

We must change the definition of what counts as religion, turning from God (the old metaphysical God, that is) to the fleeting, from eternity to time, from the long-term to the short-term, and from the inner to the outer. Religious thought has got to be not just secularized but temporalized, made immanent, mobile and expressive. We have to cause much offence, because in making these changes we have to reject much that has hitherto been highly regarded. Consider these verses from no. 61, 'Vertue', in George Herbert's *The Temple*:[5]

> Sweet day, so cool, so calm, so bright,
> The bridall of the earth and skie:
> The dew shall weep thy fall to night;
>   For thou must die.
> Sweet rose, whose hue angrie and brave
> Bids the rash gazer wipe his eye:
> Thy root is ever in its grave,
>   And thou must die.
> Sweet spring, full of sweet days and roses,
> A box where sweets compacted lie;
> My musick shows ye have your closes,
>   And all must die.
> Onely a sweet and vertuous soul,
> Like season'd timber, never gives;
> But though the whole world turn to coal,
>   Then chiefly lives.

Reading this recently I was grieved to think that something so exquisitely beautiful should be such an odious lie. For it is. Virtuous souls die, too: we know that. Worse, virtues themselves also die. We know that, too. So nothing is in any position to look down upon the merely mortal.

The poem makes us aware of the extent to which our entire culture has been founded on a falsehood, the falsehood which claims that something is immortal, and then goes on to say that mortal beauties are by contrast merely skin-deep, tempting certainly, but treacherous and in the end emptied of worth by their own transience. Real, lasting value and intelligibility were hiked out of this world altogether. Result – the body and this present life came to be regarded with that extraordinary blend of lyrical sadness, nostalgia, pagan yearning, malignant resentment and deep suspicion which is still our psychological inheritance and burden. And which colours Herbert's text, poisoning all its sweetness.

I wanted to begin by saying that Herbert's poem, first published in 1633, dates from almost the last period when an artist could make a flawlessly beautiful work out of a traditional platitude, without feeling a fool. But the work is not flawless. At least, it's not self-consistent, because it is all too eloquent in its praise of the sensuous beauty that it describes, exemplifies – and yet condemns. Read the poem two or three times, and you will find that you know the first verse by heart well before you know the last. As so often, the very work that tells us to ascribe real value only to timeless and incorruptible things is itself highly sensuous, emotionally disturbing and timebound. Herbert creates his effects and conveys his message by luxuriating in precisely what he is telling us to avoid. He is stepping deep into the pagan lyrical tradition and using it, supposedly, to reject it in favour of Christian values. How can a work so aesthetic manage to be religious, when it is so busy assuring us that the aesthetic, being ephemeral, is irreligious?

Herbert's problem is already surfacing in Plato's attitude to art. Music, painting, poetry and so on are all of them purely sensuous.

They operate entirely in the world of appearances. Which means, surely, that there cannot be art with a serious philosophical or religious message? The only correct view of art has to be that to which Islam has come nearest. Serious philosophy and religion have to be austere and iconoclastic. Art is relegated to the status of a tolerated parallel secular tradition, where it is associated with decoration, dalliance, entertainment, diversion and harmless pleasure. It can be very polished, but it does not pretend to be adequate to express the central themes of the faith.

Unfortunately this position is not consistent, either. Sermons appeal to the emotions, just as much as do secular love-songs. Scripture is sensuous, too. Grand and austere geometrical sacred architecture works upon our feelings just as much as curvy Art Nouveau does. The fact is that if the great themes of religion and philosophy are to be articulated within our human world at all, then they have got to be expressed in the sensual and the transient. Human life as such is inescapably aesthetic and sensuous. Consistent asceticism and otherworldliness are not in fact possible.

Thus the inconsistency we now detect in Herbert is but one illustration of a flaw running throughout our whole tradition, a fault that we can no longer conceal from ourselves. The enormous ideological effort of the past, which erected a Real World of God, eternity and the rest beyond the world of appearances, was in its day perhaps a necessary fiction. It did a job. Yes, we are even grateful to it. But now we see clearly that it was radically incoherent. There is only the transient flux of language-formed, feeling-coloured experience. The notion of something else 'behind' it all isn't even statable. There is nothing behind these lines of words that I am writing down for you, and there is nothing behind the stream of language-formed events.

Thus we urgently need a true religion of the fleeting moment and the slipping-away meaning. A first hint of what it might be like can be gleaned from the Japanese poet Matsuo Bashō (1644-1694).[6] In his middle years Bashō seems to have passed through something of a psychological crisis, which turned him towards Zen Buddhism. In the spring of 1689 he sold his house and set off on foot to walk through the primitive North of the country. As he went along he wrote poems, which he incorporated into a delicately-beautiful little travel-book. His translator explains: 'the Narrow Road to the Deep North was life itself for Bashō, and he has travelled through it as anyone would travel through the short span of his life here – seeking a vision of eternity in the things that are, by their own very nature, destined to perish. In short, *The Narrow Road to the Deep North* is Bashō's study in eternity, and in so far as he has succeeded in this attempt, it is also a monument he has set up against the flow of time.'[7]

Those are the words of Noboyuki Yuasa, Bashō's accomplished translator, who is doubtless trying to interpret the poet's message to a Western audience. But he misleads us. Bashō is no platonist. He nowhere uses words like 'eternity', and he never evokes anything unchanging. He concentrates, in a very clear and objective way, on some feature of the world of experience, *and nothing else*:

> Breaking the silence
> Of an ancient pond,
> A frog jumped into water –
> A deep resonance.

A *haiku*, remember, is a seventeen-syllable poem with a 5-7-5 structure. Here the frog jumps into the water, *glop*, in the central section. The opening and closing words wrap that event in a skin of subjectivity, by alluding to the profound silence before, and a very faint hollowness in the ears for a moment after, the frog's leap. The sound is a little reverberant, almost bell-like: – – – – Glop –p –p – – –.

Nothing in this poem need be called 'a vision of eternity', whatever that might be. Rather, it turns upon the old Zen theme of the unity of subjectivity and objectivity: a disciplined and responsive attention to experience, perfectly articulated in words. Bashō describes the emotional colouring of a poem by using the word *sabi*, loneliness. D.T. Suzuki went a little further and

16

proposed the phrase 'eternal loneliness' as a translation. But this again, surely, is to platonize Bashō. The poet is not talking about eternity in the Western sense which opposes it to things temporal and sensuous. On the contrary, he's talking about what it takes to do full justice to time and 'the floating world'. My subjectivity must become, as it were, religiously cleansed and disciplined if my feeling-response to experience is to be deep, clear and true. It took many years of hard self-schooling to get that frog as right as Bashō gets it; and to get it that right is religion.

On his *Narrow Road* Bashō arrived at Kanazawa to find that the poet Isshō was dead and buried. Bashō attended the memorial service at Isshō's graveside:

> Move, if you can hear,
> Silent mound of my friend,
> My wails and the answering
> Roar of autumn wind.

We know that there will not be any movement in response, for death, human mourning and the wind's cry are all alike just natural events and no more. And yes, that is a sort of ... consolation.

Bashō ends his little book not by coming to rest, but by moving on again. The last lines of the text are another *haiku*:

> As firmly cemented clam-shells
> Fall apart in autumn,
> So I must take to the road again.
> Farewell, my friends.

And he was to continue wandering for two more years before returning to Edo. In his late forties now, he was an old man: his contemporary the poet-painter Buson portrays him as small, wizened and cheerful. In fact, he often had to struggle hard against depression. But I am emphasizing that his work cannot be read as 'a quest for eternity' in the Western and platonic sense. On the contrary, it is in more than one way a celebration of transience:

of his own journey, of the self's transitoriness and of transient experience.

The poet is reconciled to transience. Indeed he disappears into it, for the way the poems work depends upon acceptance of the transience of the self. We can see this if we take a little further the theme of the reciprocity of objectivity and subjectivity, which we mentioned previously. The younger Bashō had sometimes been a little too wayward and self-indulgent in his verses. To get that frog just right Bashō must empty and clarify his mind, holding it still and calm as the pond, so that the full objectivity of the frog's *glop* can enter into and express itself within his subjectivity. The poem is a little chain of signs just seven words long, no more. Like the surface of the pond, the chain of signs has two faces, an upper and a lower. The upper face is a transient world-event: the frog hits the pond, *glop*. Below the water-surface, as it were, the underside of the poem is a receptive movement of responsive feeling within the poet's subjectivity. When the poem is just right, perfectly harmonized and balanced, the self disappears. It has become completely receptive, conformed, transparent to the natural event. The poem remains as an amen, let it be.

There is no platonism in this, no revelation of the eternal world 'in, with and under' the frog's *glop*. Bashō sits by the pond. We are told by a pupil who was present that it was a mild dampish day in late March. A pigeon cooed, and one or two petals of cherry-blossom fell. An event impinges upon Bashō's consciousness. You may read it as a musical note, but to me it sounds like a *glop*. I'm hearing it too. Listen. You can, as well.

There are now six elements in the philosophical situation. Bashō's alert sensibility is like a flat surface or diaphragm (1). An event (2) impinging upon this surface produces from beneath the diaphragm a subjective feeling response (3) in Bashō. It moves over the surface as a ripple (4); but a ripple of what? To become a heard intelligible sound it needs to be read as a sign (5) which can then activate other signs.[8] The disciple Shiko (1665–1731), who was present, reports that Bashō himself came up with the words

18

A frog jumped into water –
A deep resonance.

There was some further consultation and reflection before Bashō completed his poem (6).

The poem began with the activation of a sign. Analysing backwards and then reconstructing how the *haiku* got written, we have found (1) a surface; (2) an impinging event; (3) a subjective feeling-response; (4) a ripple beginning to move on the surface; and (5) the codification of the ripple as a sign. Once the sign has arrived we've got a little scrap of conscious, meaningful experience. A word, a thought. Logos has begun to move. One word leads to another: *glop*, water, frog. And Bashō is now composing by selecting from the sign-sequences running back and forth on the surface.

Bashō's responsiveness to experience and his literary craftsmanship thus become as it were his preparation for death. His religiousness is the calm and self-effacement with which he lets the transient be itself within himself – and his self disappears, leaving behind a small finished work of literary art.

What now do we make of the claim that Bashō in his middle age seeks a vision of eternity, and sets up a monument against the flow of time? Until someone says more plainly just what 'a vision of eternity' is supposed to be, I shall go on thinking that Bashō has given us nothing but a scrap of contingent experience, perfectly articulated in words in a way that catches the heart. There wasn't any extra object around that Bashō overlooked or somehow failed to incorporate into his poem. On the contrary, Bashō has said it all. All of it.

And that's eternity. It's all that eternity *can* be. An art-unity of word and feeling in the passing moment, with which one is content. The frog hits the water, *glop*, and a little poem takes shape in Bashō's mind.

Does that give a hint of how there might be a religion of transience, free from the illusion and time-hate we know too well?[9] Of course our own enquiry is not going to lead us quite to

Bashō's outlook. But we will be doing very well if we can come up with something as free from untruth as his little book.

2

PARTS, NOT SOULS

When we think about the appearance-reality distinction, we start by thinking it outwards. We imagine ourselves in a situation like that of the prisoners in Plato's Cave. Before us there is a screen. On the screen there is maybe a text, a diagram, or a pattern of flickering appearances. It is something immediately accessible to us: either a bit of language or theory, or a bit of the world of appearance. It is supposed to be a reflection or representation of the way things are in the unseen Real World, out on the far side of the screen. Unfortunately, we never get a good unimpeded look at the Real World, though we are told that it is of a quite different order from the world of appearance; and we do not know for sure what system of projection or set of mapping-conventions links the world in representation to the unseen Real World beyond. So the prisoners in the Cave are justified in being sceptical. We concluded therefore that the appearance-reality distinction is a menace. Once it gets established in a culture it seems to go on for ever, causing one philosophical illness after another. It's time we were rid of it. Instead of looking for an exit from the Cave or trying to cure the prisoners' scepticism, we ought to be refusing to get involved with the picture of ourselves as stuck in the Cave in the first place.

This means that we should not allow the split between the apparent – whether it be sense-experience, or language or theory or images – and the Real ever to open up. It makes for more sense and fewer problems to regard the continuum of language-formed events as being just one layer thick. We won't try to split it between fact and interpretation, matter and mind, things and words, appearance and Reality or whatever. Our world is always already verbalized, articulated, made ours. Morality? – a matter of the feeling-tones and valuations currently annexed to words. Religion? – to be identified with its own stories, images and practices. God is the Divine Names. And so on; there is nothing extra hidden from view. What you see is all there is.

Yet all this is only half the story. I said that we tend to begin by thinking the appearance-reality distinction outwards, as Plato does. Reality is postulated as being out on the far side, not within and on the hither side, of the screen. No doubt this is because we are natural realists, who like to project out, spatialize and objectify the Real. And I have suggested that there are gains to be made by first going along with this way of setting up the issue, and then criticizing it. We come to see why we should refuse to accept the outward-moving appearance-reality distinction, for it devalues and relativizes the manifest world, and creates insoluble problems of knowledge. But there are even greater gains to be made by examining and criticizing the inward moving appearance-reality distinction as well – and then putting the two critiques together.

The inward-moving distinction has also come to us from the Greeks. It is the familiar contrast between 'the outer man' and 'the inner man', as St Paul calls them.[1] Body and Soul. The empirical self and the noumenal self. The public self and the private self. The social self that interacts with other human beings in this world, and the immortal core-self that relates itself only to the eternal world. The self that other people can see, the apparent self, is a living, moving body that acts in the world, speaks, loves and works, grows old and dies. But we are also said to have an inner first-person life, the life of our individual subjective thinking consciousness, and some of us hope that this private mental life of ours may continue after death. A sharp outer-inner dualism suggests that the inner self is the Real self, a distinct and independent entity like a spirit, and therefore perhaps able to live and function apart from the body and the human social world. The history here is a little confused, especially by the development from the immortal soul of the Middle Ages to the subjective consciousness of more recent times.[2] But undoubtedly the appear-ance-reality distinction, between an outer self and a real inner self, has been prolonged in the West because of the encouragement it gives to our individualism and to our hopes for life after death.

St Augustine's immortal rational soul, the genuine article, survived until as recently as a generation ago. It was a finite thinking substance that was highly aware of existing *coram Deo*, which means that it faced God all the time and developed its relation to God through a wide range of religious acts. You were acutely aware of living on the outskirts of eternity. Year by year you said the same words, experienced the same divine Grace, and related yourself to God by the same acts. It was *déjà vu, déjà vu*; your identity was repeatedly confirmed by God's own eternal self-sameness. Time kept on circling round, and returning you into your own Origin.

In those days people in general lacked the idea that *a priori* reasoning, conscience and sense-experience were historically-conditioned and theory-laden. It seems strange in retrospect, but we were simply not deeply imbued with cultural relativism. Our own thinking seemed to us natural and innocent. And this presumption of innocence was especially strong in respect of the relation to God. After all, in your relation to God you had drawn aside for a while from 'the world'. Before God there could be no question of dressing up, role-play, artifice or deception. Only pure truth was possible. Your mind was completely exposed to God, who read your inmost thoughts. So you assumed that your own religious experiences must be epistemologically uncontaminated. They were to be taken at face value. It certainly never struck me that my own religious experiences were datable cultural products, which any competent historian of religion could place as easily as an antique dealer places a piece of porcelain. As I say, the ideology of the immortal soul before God acted to fend off the thought that our religious experiences are and must be formed by our own historically-evolved religious beliefs.

Morality was similarly hiked out of history and culture, at least for believers, because our whole moral life was managed under the general heading of the relation to God. You were accountable to God, and after your death you faced a thorough Audit by him. God ran morality, which therefore participated in his own objectivity and timelessness.

It might be thought – and indeed today certainly would be thought – that just by using language in prayer, and in particular language shaped by human power-relations and human sexuality, you were inevitably ensuring that your God-relationship was intertwined with things cultural and contingent. Yet we did not recognize the point. Although one did use human language and imagery to frame and guide the various acts of prayer, thought as such was supposed to be non-linguistic, and communication with God seemed to be by a special kind of spiritual telepathy. It thus avoided the treacherousness and ambiguity of all merely human exchanges. God was as completely straight with you as you were compelled to be with him. He saw exactly what you were, and in what respects you fell short of what he had predestined you to be. He knew just what remedial treatment you required, and he alone could administer it. No wonder, then, that the relation to God seemed so innocent. The teasing uncertainty that colours all ordinary human relations simply could not enter it.

Thus everything that was most important about you – the definition of your identity, the knowledge of your true moral condition, your most necessary relationship, and the way to your true selfhood and eternal happiness – was all located in an inner metaphysical realm. It was a kind of theatre of true selfhood, but quite independent of 'the world' – i.e., of language, culture, history and everyday human relationships. This inner realm of the Real self was noumenal. By comparison with it, the whole of your outer life was mere appearance.

As I have been suggesting, the whole system was kept in place chiefly by two principles. The first was the very sharp ideological distinction between Real divinely-ordained things and things that rested only on the shifting sands of human convention. Hence the familiar oppositions: religion/culture, revelation/human reason, unchanging divine truth/changing human theories. Contrasts such as these delayed our realizing that all religious terms, ideas and experiences really are human historical products (and, indeed, couldn't *not* be so). The second principle that helped to sustain the soul was the belief in thought. Thought was pictured as an invisible spiritual activity that went on in a special non-spatial sort of inner space, the mind, which was somehow linked to the brain. The mind was a command-and-control centre, a small spotlight of subjective consciousness within the body.

The queerest contradiction was this. The mind's various doings and goings-on were all represented in a special mentalistic vocabulary. This lexicon was entirely made up of metaphors drawn from ordinary physical acts of operating, seeing, grasping, taking and so on. Words such as concept, abstract, comprehend, intuit and so forth show that the mind is just an abstracted Latin ghost of the body. That is, just the very words we use to talk about the mind make it clear that the mind is a secondary cultural construction, a tower of metaphors. Our subjectivity, our feeling that we have an inner life, is a special kind of cultural artefact made of linguistic idioms, and nothing else. Mind is a cultural fiction.

However, the whole point of building this delicate artefact, the mind and our religious subjectivity, was that it should come to be take for granted by one and all as being primary, founding, metaphysical, non-linguistic and utterly Real. By an act of unconscious legerdemain, culture in the past contrived to make its most highly-artificial products appear the most completely natural, so that they seemed to be independently real. Logic, conscience, thoughts, the soul, God: we did not think of these things as cultural products. They seemed to be unchanging, part of the order of things.

During the present century, though, and especially since the rise of the fully-developed global consumer and media society, we have at last become aware of culture. The *OED* Supplement suggests that in Britain, snobbish and backward as always, 'culture' still meant high culture only, even as late as the 1950s. The modern use of the word culture appears to date, in the

English-speaking world, from the early 1960s. Culture as the mental programming shared by all members of a society, culture as a system of signs, culture as very nearly identifiable with the common language. And it is above all this latter concept of culture that decisively and finally resolves the human being down into language and history. We are not fully distinct individual substances any longer, and there is no transcendent or unseen part of us. We are entirely immanent, that is we are fully immersed in our cultural context. We are no longer dual beings; we do not transcend ourselves any longer. We are our lives, and our lives are our various interactions, relationships and roles. So we are highly interwoven with others. I am like a rippling motion, a pattern held for a while, in the continuously flowing stream of events that is the world of everyday life. We are all making ourselves up all the time. Culture provides a large vocabulary, a phantasmagoria of images and a huge repertoire of roles and stories. This great wardrobe is always in motion, rotating around the place, always to hand. We grab a bit of it as it goes past. Eclectically, we put together the various selves and characters that we feel like presenting to the world. Like models on a catwalk, or like the admirable popular entertainer Madonna, we change our dress and our self-presentation pretty frequently. A person has become merely a personality, a mask, and improvised role. Nowadays we are all parts, not souls. Bits of the flood.

Is all this a comedown? Well, it's happened. We see now that our world is an endless river of signs and interpretations. Thinking has become just a part of the process of the world, visible on people's faces and audible in what they say. When I impute thoughts or a mind to you, I'm just reading visible signs. I read you like a book, I really do; and I guess you can probably read me better than I can read myself. For thinking is no longer anything private and spiritual over and above the movement of signs in which it is transacted. It simply is that movement. These present sentences, lines of words, are specimens of thinking. What you see, this chain of marks, the best I can do, is all there is. I have nothing in reserve. I am not *able* to mean more than what these marks are. The marks are just themselves, and an interpretation of their meaning cannot consist in anything but a few more of the same.

If we can thus learn to locate thought on the body-surface, then we can learn to avoid making the mind-body distinction. We won't see the mental as occupying a special sort of hidden inner space within the body. Instead, 'the mind' will become just a culture-guided way of reading bodily motions. As we daily bump into each other, we learn to cope with each other by learning to recognize recurrent patterns in each other's behaviour. A facial expression, a gesture, a bit of body-language, a cry – these things become readable signs by which we can orient our behaviour towards each other. Language is then a further elaboration of the same communicative and interpretative skills. So I live on my surface and in my communicative interactions, and am woven into our world.

Now I perceive the folly of the old notion that knowing something consists in having an inner mental model of it, a map or picture or snapshot in one's head. For not only is there nowhere for knowledge thus conceived to be, but this theory of what knowledge is does no explaining. It is a residue of the type of primitive thought that is explained by postulating a spirit-duplicate. The soul as a ghostly replica of the body, knowledge as a ghostly copy of its object. That such explaining-by-duplication does no work is made clear when we consider that merely to possess a map, a circuit-diagram or a balance-sheet is not of itself to know anything. You have to know how to use these things. The knowing consists in the possession and exercise of that skill – which is something publicly teachable, overt and behavioural. Postulating additional inner diagrams and records and inner skills of consulting and using them does not get us any forrader. To take a simple and homely illustration, I can teach you to find your way around Cambridge. I can also teach you the skill of using a map of Cambridge to find your way around. But there is no way I can teach you, and in any case I don't need to teach you, how to form and consult an inner mental representation of Cambridge.

So it is quite sufficient for us to be pragmatists about knowledge and truth.

It follows from all this that the one and only myth that we really do need to give up is philosophy's own founding myth, the myth of transcendence, the myth that myth can somehow be left behind, the myth of spirit, thought and mind. The myth that the real meaning and truth of a thing can be found by resorting to something extra, and hidden within or behind it. We have been animists from the first beginnings of humanity until only the day before yesterday. But now all is changed.

The realization of how radically we humans are immersed in the horizontal flow of history and culture and language may be considered threatening. The reason is that self-consciousness in our tradition has always been represented as supernatural, and as requiring a two-layered ontology. To be self-conscious, it has seemed, you need to be a spiritual substance distanced from culture and society, and coming to know yourself in and through your relation to God. But since about the time of Hegel, since (that is) about 1805, all that old metaphysics has been collapsing. The self has become naturalized within the flow of time and history. The former route to self-consciousness seems to be closed.

The word 'conscious', literally 'co-knowing', implies a certain dualism. Some higher-level element within the self looks down upon and controls a lower-level element. So what does the modern secularization of mind and self-consciousness do to the dream of pursuing the maximum degree of clear consciousness of ourselves and our world? Are we now to disappear into the temporal flux of narrative, myths and dreams?

No; but it has to be acknowledged that consciousness has changed. The older sort of consciousness depended upon a metaphysics of finite and infinite spiritual substances, and upon the notion of pure thought, independent of language and cultural conditioning. But we now see that that spirituality was only ever a rhetorical structure, a narrative constructed *within* language. This punctures our ancient illusions. We find ourselves obliged to return chastened into narrativity and the flux of linguistic signs.

28

There is nothing but the passage of time and the movement of meaning down the chain of signs. The chain of signs is always narrative. Its movement does two jobs simultaneously: it forms objective experience into a world, and it evokes the subjective play of desire. Thus by its motion language sets us too in motion, and gives us a life in a world.

But have we lost old-style spiritual self-consciousness? No: the Enlightenment project may have looped the loop. It may have gone through a stomach-churning inversion. But it is still on course. With the loss of the illusion that we may be able ontologically to transcend this illusory world, consciousness ceases to be spiritual and becomes instead ironical. The shift is considerable. The older Augustinian sort of spiritual self-consciousness involved non-linguistic thought, pure and naked truth, and unambiguous communication. The newer sort of ironical and reflective self-consciousness is more like a Jewish joke. It is highly languagey. It doubles back upon itself. It does not shun, but is actually an effect of the ambiguity and endlessness of language. It is not solemn and straight but playful, and not substantial but flickering.

Yes, we see now that signs are only signs and myths are only myths, and that we must be content with them. Instead of the old, old platonic illusion of Truth, we now have the truth of illusion. I am not a sovereign immortal spirit that is or hopes to be self-transparent and self-possessed. All I am is a transient flickering irony that colours the motion of these signs.

I like it that way. I am not complaining, and I am not sunk in myth either. The newer type of reflective self-consciousness is in fact very intense. Yes, it is only an effect of the movement of words. But remember that from the new point of view the older type of spiritual self-consciousness was also only a literary effect. We are not worse off. In fact we are better off, because we are less deceived. The changeover, from the old metaphysical to the new literary view of the world, is a significant historical advance. I feel freer and clearer for having made it. I am not going back: that really would be a cop-out. No, we must go on. We'll find in the end that we really are doing better. I prefer the new regime, and I am not nostalgic for the old. Join me.

So we shall not postulate a hidden metaphysical reality beyond the flux of language-formed events, and we shall not postulate a metaphysical subject on the hither side of it either. The primary object that we start from and which we do not divide is the flux of language-formed events, within which all else is constructed. Now we have to elaborate in more detail this new vision of the human situation.

3

THE SIX TRUTHS

Our view of the human situation is still to this day confused by the persisting influence of bad and misleading old metaphors. One of the very worst goes back to Plato.[1] It sees all of our visual experience as being like viewing images flickering on a screen. The metaphor prompts us to develop two different ideas. One is that our visual experience must be second-hand and unsatisfactory because we do not see things themselves, but only images of them. The other idea insinuated by Plato's metaphor is that just as we might persuade a child to switch off the television and pay attention to something else more substantial, so the same eyes that view the screen of visual experience generally might be able to turn aside from it and look directly at the Real.[2]

But have you ever gone round the back to see what's on the far side of the screen of visual experience? Of course you haven't, because the supposition is incoherent. It has you taking your power of vision with you as you go to look behind the-screen-of-all-that-is-visible. But the initial hypothesis put everything visible on the screen and tied you up, permitting you to see only the screen. The point of this was to assert that human visual powers are screen-directed only. There is not and there cannot be anything that is visible but off-screen, for the screen is a metaphor for the entire visual field.

The strange and sinister power of Plato's screen-metaphor is that it seems to keep whispering to us that these eyes of ours are capable of a more direct and higher kind of vision than this, while also making it clear that that hope is incoherent. Plato fills the soul with an impossible, poisonous longing. He always has done.

31

The same paradox arises in relation to our seemingly incurable desire to talk our way out of language altogether – as if people just cannot absorb the fact that terms like transcendent, ineffable, beyond language and so on remain firmly within language. When the ineffable has been referred to, it has been effed.

In these cases we cling obstinately to the illusion-generating metaphor because we somehow hate the thought of radical immanence, contingency and outsidelessness. We simply cannot get our minds around it. But we've got to try. If we can see why it's useless to dream of looking behind the screen of the visual field, and if we can see why it is futile to try to talk our way beyond the reach of language, then perhaps we can grapple with the notion that meaning and truth have become completely immanent. That is, they both belong within the realm of human communication. Meanings depend entirely upon expectations aroused by regularities in our behaviour towards each other. Meanings are just human usages. Meanings are just customs, done things. So there is no sense in postulating any objective meaning, out there beyond the world of human communicative interactions. Meanings, just as much as fashions, are wholly immanent within the flow of human life and feeling. And truth is similarly immanent, so completely tied up with our human procedures for establishing it, determining it, testing it and agreeing upon it that there is no point in trying to push the notion of truth out beyond the realm of human communication.

Easily said; and one can begin to glimpse where it might lead. To, approximately, the world-view of the novel. A world made of language, a radically humanistic world, a world of social exchange. But it remains very difficult to go the whole way. We seem to keep on wanting something extra. So persistent are the old illusions of objectivity, reality and the like that I have doubts about whether Hilary Putnam's human realism (*Realism with a Human Face*, as he calls it[3]) is sufficiently strongly-worded to exorcise them. He uses the phrase 'internal realism' to summarize his view, clearly right, that issues of reality, truth and the like do at least get raised, rationally debated and resolved *within* the world of human communication. This, then, is a realism internal to the human realm. The only thing that we must try to shut out is the old mythical idea that Reality and Truth can be or need to be projected out beyond the world of human communication and gives some sort of independent existence and grounding. We need to replace the old metaphysical realm, which has recently collapsed, with an American-style pragmatic humanism.

Thus far Putnam, and he's not wrong. But does he put it sufficiently forcefully to banish the old errors? I doubt it. We may need also to employ some more active purge, for example by using an anti-Plato story to combat Plato's story.[4] Like this, perhaps:

We live in a windowless house that we have made ourselves. We are constantly altering it, pushing back the walls, redesigning it. We have opened up this space around ourselves by developing our language, our culture and our knowledge-systems. It is a semantic space, big enough by now to make a very rich and complex life possible within it. But we never get outside. There are people who claim that the house does have an outside. They argue that we have gone so far by now in opening up the interior that we can safely presume that the exterior of the house is of about the same shape as the inside. This view is called by its proponents 'critical realism'. The adjective is quite undeserved, for the hypothesis is once again incoherent. Imagine that you are in some deep underground cavern: it is not possible to dig your way out, because all your efforts to break through to the exterior merely have the effect of enlarging the interior. And that is how it is with this house. Trying to push through the walls, you can succeed only in pushing them back. We cannot get out of our own knowledge, our own world. This means that the 'critical realism' claim is in principle never going to be able to reach verification. It therefore does no work, and has no meaning.

I am not by this parable suggesting that we are in any way imprisoned. Of course not, for the space that we have opened up around ourselves is indefinitely extensible. It is rubbery. We can stretch it as much as we like, so there is no need at all to feel hemmed in. But (logically) there is no place for us outside our own space. Right? So we ought one day to be able to reach a point where the old illusory dream of an-outside-to-it-all no longer troubles us.

However, we are by no means at that point yet. On the contrary, we still find it extremely difficult to accept that everything is manifest, everything is interconnected and everything is internal. We are still looking for our old absolutes, dreaming of an outside, wanting support.

A consequence of the view I am trying to state is that philosophy does not have any extra information, hidden, hard-to-arrive-at and very important, to give us. There is no super-news. Dogmatic philosophy and dogmatic theology have both ended together. Henceforth philosophy, like religion, has a remedial role. It reconciles us to life by helping us to shake off our discontent. There isn't some other way things might be, in contrast with which the way things are is shown up as being very unsatisfactory. Philosophy assembles reminders of the obvious, tells us things we already know, and quotes platitudes against sophistries. Philosophy does not need to be pompous and scholastic. It needs only to be clear and effective.

So the six truths I'm going to enunciate are all extremely banal. The world is no more than what it seems to be, a continuum of language-formed experience. You and I are both fully immersed in it. Nothing transcends it either out on the far side or on the nearside, within the self. So at this stage there is no need to advert to any distinction between subjectivity and objectivity, between thought and matter, between the self and the not-self, or between Nature and Society. All those old distinctions feel a bit wrong now. I don't like them. Let's defer them, on the excellent ground that the longer you put off making a bad distinction, the less harm it does. So, when in formulating the truths we refer to 'all this' or 'everything', we incorporate the self. Consider yourself to fall wholly within the scope of what is said. And consider the six truths as working to conjure up an image of the human condition. They are too general to be internal, descriptive-type truths. Rather, they prescribe an overall vision of life. In the old phrase,

I hope it will 'convict' you. You'll have to admit that in your heart of hearts you already think this way. You'll recognize that this is how it is. At least, I hope you will.

(i)   All this is outsideless

This is the maxim of radical immanence. Everything is inside. Nothing is hidden, deep or invisible. There is no better vantage-point from which our life can be seen more clearly and judged more authoritatively than we ourselves can see and judge it. Any imagined external reality or standpoint, simply *as* something imagined, immediately relocates itself on the inside. There isn't any extra dimension of the human situation, which the film-maker or novelist are unable to show us. Life's painting is flat. People are what they look like and what they say; they are the text of their own lives. There is mystery in the sense that language and interpretation are endless, but not in the sense that there is anything occult or extra which only some people know about. To hell with experts. So far as philosophy, religion and ethics are concerned, all that is most important is manifest to everyone.

Furthermore, religion and morality, like science, are also part of the inside. Science just is its own practice and its own evolving theories. Morality is the evaluative, the emotive and action-guiding overtones currently annexed to the words of our language. Anyone who pays attention to the flavours of words in current usage can see everything that morality is. There is no metaphysical extra. Similarly, religion too is internal to the human realm. It is its own practice. The gods are just what people can be seen to be worshipping; they are our faith in them, and the things we say and feel about them and do for them. There is nothing extra. Gods have no existence outside our faith and practice. They are internal, too.

When we grasp the truth of radical immanence, then we begin to perceive the strange manner in which human institutions seem spontaneously to generate a mystique of themselves, endowing themselves with an air of transcendent mystery. They are as it were self-objectifying and self-sacralizing. The example nearest to hand is the civil law.[5] Legislatures are purely human. We do not seriously suppose that the law comes down from the world above, or that it is unchanging, or that our legislators are significantly wiser than we are. They are not. They're dumb. The continuing authority of the law is postmodern society is a puzzle, a self-generating illusion, a con-trick with no trickster. In our highly reflective society we are bound to regard the law a little ironically. It is an ass, it is a bluff, we desperately need it, it deserves our respect, we want to change it. All those things at once. Queer – but I now see religion like that, I now see morality like that, I now see just about every adjectival *thing* like that. It can't be helped. History and the social sciences have made us so ironical that we've got into the way of regarding all our great institutions as lovable, necessary old rogues, cherished hoaxes, noble lies. Don't blame me for this. It's the way we are now.

(ii)   It all just happens this way

This is the maxim of universal contingency. Everything has developed, everything is the product of time and chance, and everything just happens to have got itself set up this way. People claim that something or other is natural, or is real or is necessary; but all such talk is ideological. It is an attempt to entrench something or other as authoritative and unalterable. Maybe this is a good thing; maybe something or other fully deserves to be established as real or natural or necessary. But if so it will be we ourselves who so set it up, for all ideas about what is real or natural or necessary are our ideas, established by us, for ourselves, in one of our vocabularies. Nobody else ever told us what nature is, or what is real, or what is necessary. *We* determined these matters for ourselves, and all such determinations are contingent, for we might have determined otherwise, and we may one day change our minds.

Despite all this, there is no doubt that many people still hate the notion of universal contingency. They react sharply against it. An idealist, an absolutist, a fundamentalist is a person who takes up a stand upon some fixed point purportedly outside the flux of life, and tries to live from *that*. But it is not clear now that such people are badly deviant? They are notoriously insensitive to the relativities of life and of other people's characters and personalities. Today, by general consent, the more of relativist and contingency-person you are, the more congenial a human being you are. Besides, every sort of absolutism or fundamentalism that has yet put itself forward has proved to be merely a provincial and culturally-relative fundamentalism. It contradicts itself, claiming to offer global absolutes while in fact being merely and locally protestant, or Islamic, or whatever.

So everything is contingent, and everything is contingently interconnected by custom in such a way that everything leads on by association to everything else. Some things are conventionally or conditionally necessary, natural, real and so forth, but nothing is absolutely necessary, inescapable, foundational or finalizing.

(iii)   Meaning comes first

This is the modern and simpler version of the doctrine that philosophers used to call Idealism. Contrary to what down-to-earth, matter-of-fact, commonsense and practical Anglo-Saxons suppose, we have no good reason to believe in a fully-formed world of fact already sitting out there before we humans come along and start having ideas about it. A scientific tradition going back to Lucretius and ancient atomism pictures an objective world of inert jiggling physical particles. But those particles are theoretical entities, found in texts. Can't you see? *We* postulated them.

Look around you now. Your world is already being shaped by our own perception of it and indeed perception is and has to be saturated with theory. You see this page as paper, as white, as oblong, as a two-dimensional surface, as made of wood-pulp – in short, everything around you is plastered over with words and interpretations. There is always that screen of cultural material between us and the world; or rather, we apprehend the world not just in and through but *as* the symbols in which we represent it. Sign shapes reality. Event plus word equals experience. We get a hold of the world by interpreting it. And there is no innocent, natural, uninterpreted sense-datum. It is a world of signs. The sign comes first. The natural world around us is produced only by means of and within the cultural sign-system. I don't see the world raw; it has to be culturally cooked in order to be seen.

Now the sign is not stiff. It doesn't have all its meaning straightforwardly packed into itself. Meaning is always processual and temporal. That is, it is not contained in the sign but is produced through the motion of the sign relative to other signs. The term for this is semiosis.[6] That is what we are getting at when we say that meaning is always something behavioural, transactional, public, shifting, elusive and never completely pinned down. So the world is a heaving turbulent Sea of Meanings with many waves, currents and ripples moving across it.

The older 'phenomenalism', of which there were numerous Asian and some Western versions, reduced the world to a stream of phenomena. We see it rather as a moving field of signs, a 'post-Buddhism of the sign' or 'flux of language-formed events', as we have called it.

We have come to see the world this way during the twentieth century, as we have come to recognize how thoroughly culture shapes perception. Culture includes factors such as education, the media and advertising. Undoubtedly it profoundly influences what we single out for notice, the way we construe it and the way we feel about it. What questions this raises about our freedom, we defer for the present.

(iv)   Everything is public

We do not believe in anything metaphysical out there beyond
the flux of sign-formed events, nor do we believe in anything
metaphysical in here on the hither side of the flux of sign-formed
events. The common life-world understood as a process of sign-
formed events, comes first and embraces everything. If you want
a good representation of what it's like, see a feature film. The
feature film misses nothing out. People's thoughts, intentions,
beliefs, values and so on can all be read off the moving pictures
and the sound-track without any difficulty whatever. This makes
it clear that there is no need to take a realistic view of mind,
thoughts, values or whatever. They are simply interpretations,
and are read off the surface. They are all public. Indeed it is even
possible to dispense with the sound-track, and read people's
thoughts and characters directly off their visible behaviour in a
silent film.

You think you've got inner thoughts? But thought cannot
subsist except as a motion of signs, and signs are all of them public
objects. A sign is simply an established custom that is generally
recognized. So the alleged inner world cannot exist except as a
little fold or pouch in the surface of the public world. And if it
thus is some kind of pocket, it cannot be closed. The sign-motion
of the public world has got to be able to keep streaming in and
out of the pocket. The self cannot be sealed off. That is why,
however introverted you may fancy yourself to be, your spouse
probably still reads you better than you can read yourself. It is
because you are the patterns of readable events on your own
surface that your partner can read you like an open book.

(v)   Everything is historical

This is the maxim of dialectical humanism. Nothing's fixed, self-
present and self-contained: it cannot be. But everything slowly
changes together. A slice across the whole sign-system as it is at
any one time will reveal a fairly coherent cultural totality.[7] By

that I mean, a construal of the world, a set of practices and a valuation of life. Nothing says that it all has to be tightly systematic, and it seldom or never is so; but it does all have a characteristic period flavour. Thus, for the British, everything Early Victorian has a strong and distinctive Early Victorian period flavour to it. Read Dickens or John Stuart Mill. But this is not to say that people in Early Victorian times were all the same, or that they were notably self-consistent individuals. Of course they were not. Nevertheless, they do share that period flavour or style. Hegel called it the *Zeitgeist*, and Hazlitt compared it with the prevailing climate of a place.

However, culture is not a fixed thing. It is always already in motion. The rules are slowly changing, the goal-posts are shifting. We don't shift them by our own individual will. They are sustained and they can be shifted only through the interplay of forces in the public domain. That's historical change.

(vi) *Nothing says it must all add up*

Otherwise put, there is no pre-established harmony between thought and being. Nothing says either that there have to be answers to our questions, or that whatever answers there are have got to be accessible to us. Life is not obliged to make sense. The world doesn't have to be knowable. Nothing guarantees that there will ever be, or can ever be, a perfect world in which the culture is perfectly coherent, every one has reached final agreement on questions of belief and value, and history is terminated. That will never happen. If it is the case that our culture, our beliefs, our values and so forth have developed untidily, in bits and pieces and over a long period, then it is not surprising that a cultural totality should comprise a vast number of inter-related contingencies which roughly hang together, and have a common flavour – but which is not and is never likely to be tightly systematic. And because in our account we blended the self into the general flow of language-formed events in the life-world, it should be clear that what is true of the culture as a whole is true also of the social order and true also of the self.[8] Culture, society and the self are all constructed from the same continuum, so they are analogous to each other. Psychology is just sociology written small – which is why, when we lost belief in the perfectibility of the social order, we also began to lose belief in the perfectibility of the individual self. Nothing guarantees that the historical process will culminate in the emergence of a perfect society here on earth, and nothing guarantees that it is possible for the individual to achieve a state of perfect and sinless spiritual harmony and blessedness.

On this last point, Darwin and Nietzsche changed our thinking. They showed us that life is a package. Good and evil, co-operation and conflict, pleasure and pain, sickness and health, stress and relaxation, joy and affliction are all interwoven. My supposedly good impulses and my bad ones are tangled together in such a way that it is foolish to suppose that the bad impulses could simply be removed, leaving me all good. We no longer think there ever was an original perfection, either of the self or of the world, before the Fall of Man. We do not see how such a state of flawlessness could be possible, either in the past or in the future.

Where does this leave the venerable question of the meaning of life? In the old way of thinking meaning was taken to be a noun. The meaning of life would be something like a fixed formula, an answer that wrapped it all up. But I am suggesting that we should take meaning to be a participle. The meaning of life may then be seen as like the growing of grass, something that life does continuously. Semeiosis, meaning-process. The meaning of life shows in the difference between one day and the next. Life means away continuously. The temporal production of being and meaning – that is what should satisfy us. Inevitably it remains 'imperfect' in the grammatical sense – but then, our life is perfected only in death. Until we die, we should go on saying yes to imperfection and uncompletedness.

4

LIFE TIME

The six truths, then, are as follows. *All this is outsideless* (radical immanence). *It all just happens this way* (universal contingency). *Meaning comes first* ('culturalism' or 'superstructuralism'). *Everything is public. Everything is historical.* And, finally, *Nothing says it must all add up* (i.e. language is only human, and there is no external guarantee of either meaning or value or systematic coherence). Outsidelessly, the world is a continuous stream of language-formed events – goings-on, communications, interactions, displays, narratives. It is an historically-evolved human social product, untidy, contingent, guaranteeing nothing; but it is what we have. It is the world that represents itself to itself in such media as the newspaper, the feature film and the novel. It is a world of symbolic exchange – of conversation, rituals and trade – and it is the matrix within which everything else is produced.

Such is the vision of the world with which, most of the time, people now operate. They may, they do, profess a great variety of other views, but their actual behaviour is based on this one.

The new world view is not quite the same as the dialectical humanism pioneered by Hegel, which for much of the modern period has flourished in both conservative and socialist forms.[1] Dialectical, organic humanism means an historical and social humanism, a humanism of social roles and social exchanges. It is opposed to individualism and to all abstract and essentialist notions of human nature. What we are, we have become in society, and within an historically-evolved tradition. And thus far we applaud dialectical humanism and agree with it. Yes, the self is

42

public. It is the social person. That is, it exists in its expression: hence my 'expressionism'. We are our lives, that is, our own living of them. We are our enactment of our social roles, we are our dealings with others. We are our own changes over time. My reflexive self-consciousness is not to be taken as evidence that I have or am an extra-historical 'substance', an unchanging metaphysical soul. On the contrary, self-awareness is an historical product which does a social job. It is a sort of pleat, where part of my outer surface is folded back upon itself and comments a little wryly upon itself. But this ironical self-awareness is a very fluctuating phenomenon, and less important than used to be supposed. It does not make very much difference to the world. The torrent of public cultural life goes on regardless and, frankly, does not need to take individual subjectivity too seriously. It goes its own way. So dialectical humanism, yes – but. The nineteenth-century dialectical humanists were much more optimistic and teleological in outlook than we can be. They did not yet feel compelled to accept either the universal contingency thesis or the absence of guarantees. So they were not yet troubled by the thought of the mortality of values. They could afford to be cheerful about the long-term prospects for the race. They saw history as a progressive objectification of reason. This meant at the very least that the to-and-fro of human interactions would gradually tend to overcome contradictions and procure reconciliation. In the longest run the world must become more and more coherent, rational and reconciled. Thus people felt entitled to expect that everything would eventually add up, everything was going to make sense. All the loose ends would be tied in, and nothing would be utterly wasted.

In all this the dialectical humanists were far more metaphysically optimistic than we can be. They were confident that a universally reconciled and benign state of the world was possible (it *could* all add up), and they were confident that the dark tangle of human struggles and conflicts is not merely tragic and futile, but sorts itself out and steers itself towards a favourable outcome (something is at work to ensure that in the end it *will* all add up).

43

There was a side of the angels to be on. People felt reasonably confident that the self was stably self-possessed, self-aware and the subject of rights. Even if it was not quite the metaphysical substance it had once been, its life was at least woven into and part of the life of coherent and ongoing totalities. It was capable of effective historical action lastingly to realize lasting values embodied in a reconciled and coherent social organism. A self therefore capable of personal integration and fulfilment; a self with a 'nature' that could be fully actualized through membership of a social body.

The situation of us who have been around this last thirty years or so, since the early sixties, is very different. It's not just that we have lost the belief in progress, for after all life in a stable society with stable values might be very comfortable. But we have learnt by experience that values change. Values are mortal,[2] an appalling realization that largely wipes out both the authority of the past and hope for the future. When cultural change has compelled us repeatedly to modify our beliefs and our values, we cease to be able to identify with the selves we formerly were. Nor – and this is a little harder to grasp – can we confidently envisage and identify with the selves that we hope to become. Self-perfecting ceases to be a feasible project when we find that values and beliefs no longer last a whole lifetime. This in turn weakens our belief in personal identity, and creates our very curious new situation of short-term and surface selfhood. The self itself, as well as its beliefs and values, becomes something improvised, as historical change bites into everything that once seemed to be stable and enduring.

A current example: a Conservative politician, called upon to account for a decision he took only three or four years ago, defends the action of his former self by saying: 'It was right at the time.' Right at the time. In other contexts this politician can be relied upon to speak in a suitably inspirational and objectifying way about the perennial values he and his party stand for, but when he is against the ropes he knows that yesterday's virtues are today's vices, and that values are shifting, uncertain and perspectival. Our values are not propped up or kept stable by anything outside the world of human interactions. They are as wobbly and easily-overturned as we are.

The notion that the human self is something flickering, uncertain and hastily-improvised – a fiction we make up, an act we put on, a part we play – is very unwelcome to us. We can't accept it. We feel we must struggle to establish and maintain a measure of control over our own internal affairs. To hold the self together, we need supports. We need the familiar old myths of a stable world view, an unchanging tradition, stable beliefs and values. We want pedigrees and endorsements. We are ready to go to considerable lengths in order to get all these things.

For example, we like to think that our religious beliefs go back to the very beginning of the world and earlier. We want to be able to say to ourselves: 'This is how it is, this is how it has always been, this is what has always been believed. Our way of thinking is natural and original.' Thus the doctrine of the Trinity was formulated in Christianity during the third and fourth centuries – but promptly traced back into the New Testament, the Old Testament, nay, to the very beginning of all things. And our mythicizing 'realistic' ways of thinking conceal from us the wide discrepancy between the very recent date when an idea was invented, and the primal time which it claims for its true point of origin.[3]

Is this not why our theoretical physicists put so much effort into debating cosmology and the beginning of the Universe? They seek to project their theories and their ways of thinking back to the beginning of time. In fact, the subject itself is very novel: modern physical cosmology dates back only about seventy-five years. Einstein's finite-but-unbounded model of the Universe, Edwin Hubble and the red-shift in the optical spectra of the most distant astronomical objects, the recession of the nebulae therefore, and the postulated explosion of what was then called 'the primeval atom'. These themes were taking shape in the years between the two world wars, and standard-model Big-Bang cosmology only became dominant much more recently. Yet with great energy and confidence the physicists pitch their language back to the origin of all things. They are bidding for authority, claiming in effect that their ways of thinking are natural and original, exactly as theologians used to claim. That's realism – an innocent, or maybe not-so-innocent, confidence in the objective validity and absoluteness of your own particular style of theorizing. Realists try to conquer time by pretending that their way of thinking is as old as the hills.

Now consider a more subtle example of the ways in which we may try to stabilize the self. In our thinking about time we often represent it as a linear scale on which the positions of events can be plotted, or as a great transparent container within which world events take place. But we also think of time as something that moves. Perhaps it moves like a flowing river. We are on the bank, watching time roll by. But in which direction does time move? Does it flow from the future through the present and away into the past? If so, we may think of ourselves as standing still, like a rock in the middle of a river, and looking upstream. Like the waters, time is always approaching us. As it comes level with us it becomes the present, and then slips away behind us into the past. Yet, puzzlingly, there seems to be just as good a case for seeing time as flowing in the opposite direction, from past to future. In which case we are carried along by time, heading always into the future, but suspended in a kind of bubble of motionlessness because the point where we are is always unchangingly the present. So it is as if the whole scale of linear time is like a track, and we are being conveyed along it sitting in a carriage. The length of the carriage is the bandwidth of the present. Where we are is both the point on the track that we have reached, and also the perpetual sliding present in which we live.

The motion of time from past to future can be described in a rather different vocabulary if we put the emphasis on labour and see life as the completion of a series of tasks, one after another. Like classical Hebrew and the God of Israel, we will need only two tenses, the perfect for what is already fulfilled and finished, and the imperfect for what is still pending, in hand or awaited. On this model time is a process of crystallization. Promises get fulfilled, jobs completed, decisions made. The as-yet-unformed and indeterminate future is steadily converted into the finished and unalterable past. I'm like a workman sitting at my bench, picking up, working on and completing one thing after another. I make time pass by turning a full IN-tray into a full OUT-tray.

What are we to say about these oddly-miscellaneous images? Does the future approach steadily towards me as I face it, does time carry me forward from the past and into the future, or do I myself through my activities make time go by? Or, alternatively, is time a still and unchanging scale or framework within which events take place?

If time were something other than the language in which we speak of it, we could surely check whether it flows, and if so, in what direction. But we cannot, and so it isn't. There is not a thing which is time. Dictionary definitions of time never wholly avoid circularity, because it's all a matter of words. The consciousness of time emerges only in and with the motion of signs. There is nothing to point to but the various cultural idioms, practices and chronographic devices by which time is described, measured and marked. Time is its own registration. Time is thus a cultural construction which we represent to ourselves through various metaphors. And why are the metaphors in conflict with each other? The common feature of them all is that in them time is in some way objectified or reified. It is made into a thing out there, distinct from us. It is a river rushing towards us from the future, it is a carriage bearing us forwards into the future, it is an enveloping container, it is the finishing of one task after another. The common factor underlying all these metaphors is that in each case we have managed to get time out of our own systems and have portrayed it as something external to ourselves. We picture time as something we are in, something whose motion we observe, because we want to think of ourselves as being self-identical and stable. Time goes by, but I seem to stand still. At a college reunion I think how much all these old boys have deteriorated, suppressing the thought that I'm one of them. Lying through my teeth, I flatter them that they haven't changed a bit, meaning, 'I won't admit that I have changed, and I'll do you the kindness of pretending that you haven't either (though you have).'

There is so much time-hate around, so much, and it is the legacy of philosophy, which for so long considered both that the human self at least purports to be a substance, and that substances are somehow non-temporal and metaphysical objects. But if we are radically temporal and are returned fully into time, then we are our own time. Time is the manner of our own being. We are the flux. We are just temporarily-maintained patterns. Time is life-time, which is cultural and narrative time. We don't wish to accept this. We want to make some such distinction as St Paul makes when he says, 'Though our outer nature is wasting away, our inner nature is being renewed day by day.' My outer wrappings may change; the real me inside does not change. But there is no meaningful form of that distinction. By any usable measure we are not partly temporal, but wholly temporal and temporary. And we need to come to terms with this new, fully-temporalized sort of self, fleeting all through. We would like to get hold of some fixed point, in order to feel more sure of our own reality and sanity. But there is no such fixed point. We toss on the waters, and there is no bank to which we can moor ourselves.

Buddhism's well known 'no-self' doctrine partially anticipated our modern vision. Because at the time rival faiths tended to postulate a substantial metaphysical core-self, Buddhism couched its denial of any metaphysical core-self in the form of a denial of the self as such. Today it is perhaps more religiously effective to say that people are just transient, ephemeral beings. We are cultural products. Our consciousness is an ironical effect, produced by language's bending back upon itself. But we should not take ourselves too seriously. We should look to the world, the culture. That is what comes first.

Thus we are describing a world view intermediate between realism and humanism.

The old realism said that there is a cosmos, a fully-formed and intelligible real order of things out there, independent of us. Realism said: 'There is truth out there beyond the reach of our procedures of verification. There's meaningfulness out there independent of what we mean by what we say. There's reality out there beyond what's real for us.' All this, however, I deny. For me, all thought and all intelligibility depends on language. I'm using the term 'language' in a broad sense that embraces the whole cultural sign-system, and I'm saying that we can be sure that language is only human. Meanings are made out of nothing but human interactions, habits and expectations. Meanings are just human customs, *mores*, 'ropes' as the English once called them. So meanings are just human and the only formed, and therefore, intelligible, world that there can be is a human culturally-formed world.

The late twentieth century has been the age of the media, the age of the consumer product, the age of the sign, and above all the age when a skin of scientific theory was seen to be now covering the whole of reality. The spectrum of electromagnetic radiation is fully explored, there's a full set of particles, the whole periodic table of the elements and all their chemical reactions have been investigated, and so on. My point is that we have a theory about virtually everything in sight. The whole canvas of the real is covered with paint. Culture is spread across the whole of Nature. Nothing is left bare and untouched. I am by no means suggesting that science is finished. Far from it, for I hold that we can and we will go on correcting, elaborating and even revolutionizing our scientific theory indefinitely. But we will be reworking a surface that is already fully painted over. Science works upon, not just pure Nature, but previous science. Hence our phrase 'language-formed event' for the basic constituent of the world. The world is always already an interpretation.

However, the case we have been making out against traditional metaphysical realism also destroys humanism. For all the arguments against the claim that there is a real world out there that transcends our linguistic construal of it tell equally against the notion that there's a real self in here. We reject therefore not only realism with regard to the objective world, but also realism with regard to the human subject.

Thus the world is not transcended, either outwardly by an objective intelligible order beyond experience, or inwardly by a 'strong' human subject. The self is fully immersed in its own, our own, world. And this is a very great gain. I am no longer alienated from the world. There is not any sharp distinction now between inner and outer, subject and object, event and experience. My thinking doesn't happen inside my head any more. The thought that our thinking happens inside our heads, where a spirit watches a screen, or performs queer non-physical shunting operations – all that was a cultural fiction. It belonged to a period now over. Thinking is not an enclosed interior activity any longer, and I don't need to construct any kind of secondary representation of the world in my 'mind'. No: thinking happens out in front, where my eye hits the book, and where the process of the world goes by. The world is a world of signs, a narrative-like temporal process of language-formed events, and the story of my life is a bit of its story.

Our culturalism can claim to be a modest advance on Buddhism. Let's say, rather too crudely, that Buddhist metaphysics has seen the world as an unbounded swarm of minute reciprocally-conditioning events. This formulation immediately make the relation between language and the world problematic, and indeed northern Buddhism has in general been non-realistic.[4] But on our account, because we are always already within our own language, the stream of world events is for us always already language-formed. It is so, for example, in the second sentence of this present paragraph. So we find no problem in the relation of language to reality. In the desk, the paper and the books before me now, reality is already language-formed.

The Buddhist formulation I quoted, if *per impossibile* there were some non-linguistic and extra-cultural mode of access to it, would take us into a dead universe. But for culturalism the universe, being always already interwoven with language, is alive with meaning. Religion, art and morality are still very much around – provided, that is, you accept that they have been returned into their own vocabularies and have become purely immanent. *And* changing all the time, too.

The thesis that religion and morality are purely human and quite without external support undoubtedly alarms people. It gives rise to a curious paradox, for at this point we seem to be if anything a little more sceptical than classical northern Buddhism has been. At least at the popular level, some of the major themes of Buddhist teaching seem to presuppose moral realism. It has sounded as if we 'really' do have a moral world order, permanent moral values and a permanently open path to a blissful Release from suffering ready laid out for us.

So the difference boils down to this. In metaphysics our cultural- ism is a little bit more self-consistent and affirmative than Buddhist phenomenalism. But in moral philosophy Buddhist thought sounds rather more realistic than we can be. Our acknowledgment that values really are mortal is very tough. It requires us continually to reimagine and reaffirm our values just in order to keep them alive. We are compelled to keep on actively creating our own way out of trouble. We must run to stand still, swim to stay afloat. The Buddha did not foresee a situation quite as extreme as that, but it is the position we are in. Active non-realism, the new religion.

5

THE WORLD OF SIGNS

(i) Signs of life

Animals communicate, but there are some problems of definition.[1] Sometimes an animal's behaviour can mean something to another animal without being a genuine communication. A cricket moves. To a nearby frog that movement means food, so the frog snaps it up. Did the cricket then communicate with the frog, albeit inadvertently? No, it did not. I don't need to talk in any teleological way about what the cricket did or did not 'mean' to do. It is sufficient to say that the cricket's movement cannot be read as doing a useful biological job *for the cricket*.

A communicative expression, I shall argue, has to be a sort of speech-act. It must have a biological rationale, and it must have the properties of a sign. The message the cricket sends out isn't a real message unless it is in some way good for the cricket.

We begin, then, with this formulation: among animals a sign is a little behavioural display that causes another animal to modify its behaviour in a manner biologically advantageous to the first animal.

That covers most of the obvious cases, such as warning displays, deceptions, threats, territorial proclamations, courtship, pair-bonding rituals, begging for food, dominance and submission behaviours and so on. Notice in all this that we just can't help reading animal behaviours as speech-acts, under the general rubric that their 'meaning' just is their biological rationale – with the corollary, it seems, that human speech acts similarly have a biological rationale. We cannot survive unless we can modify the behaviour of others a little, to our own advantage: and speech is for *that* purpose. It procures co-operation.

A question arises about seeming cases of animal altruism. A monkey stands sentinel for a feeding group of adults and young, his troupe. An eagle glides down. The monkey successfully gives the alarm call, and the group scatters to hide deep in the brushwood – but the sentinel himself falls prey to the eagle. How can such a behaviour have evolved, if it is to the sentinel's own disadvantage?

No doubt orthodox darwinism can give various replies. Since the sentinel monkey is alarmed first and cannot hear his own cry later than others hear it, he must surely on average and in the long run have at least as good a chance of escape as the others. The troupe may actually include his genetic descendants, in which case it is to his advantage that he should fall prey and not they. And if the males generally take turns on sentry-duty, then that also will tend to level out the odds. If the sentry-institution is advantageous to the troupe as a whole, and equally hazardous to each male, then it is advantageous to each male.

The maxim is that animal signing can only have evolved if it is advantageous to the sender. It must increase the sender's chances of surviving, mating and passing on its genes. So communication exists to help you escape your enemies, beat your rivals, get a mate and raise your young. Mating itself is the central communicative action. All of which, I suggest, gives us a hint as to how intensely biological language is. For I am arguing not only that animal expressions are more language-like than most people allow, but also that human language is more biologically motivated than most people allow.

Consider the following. For an animal signing to be effective it has got to prompt just the right response in the addressee. For this to happen, the sign must have two kinds of generality. I will call them stimulus generality and use generality. Stimulus generality means that the sign's expression can tolerate a certain bandwidth of variation in the physical properties of the signifier – just as the same English sentence can be conveyed through quite a wide range of different voicings, different regional accents, different tones, pitches and so on. Use generality means that the same sign can be used to do the same kind of job on any one of an indefinitely large number of relevantly-similar occasions – just as is the case with human words.

Many social scientists strongly resist any attempt by biologists to take over their territory, and argue that the whole realm of language, the sign and cultural meanings is distinctively human. Along these lines, perhaps, Claude Lévi-Strauss's theory of 'the totemic operator' was developed to show how human beings first taught themselves to think.[2] The totem was the first universal. It symbolized the group, the class or the species. As we participate in the totem, so the individual participates in the universal, and the token in the type. Through totemism, a distinctively human institution, we taught ourselves to classify things and to make in thought the difficult transition from the individual to the universal.

This seems to make the capacity to handle universals into a purely human achievement. But I say that if animals are to develop interactive social behaviours, through which they fulfil general biological needs, then an animal has got to be able to recognize a particular behaviour by another animal as expressing a general sign, and must then move back from the generality of the sign to the particularity of its behavioural response on some one occasion.

I am not ascribing thoughts or intentions or subjective consciousness to animals. As we have seen, I want so far as possible to avoid dualism both in the human case and in the animal. All I'm claiming is that we have as much reason for saying that animal behaviours presuppose the ability to handle cases as instances of general rules as we have for saying that human behaviours do. Furthermore, we can just as easily recognize the kind of 'speech-act' that an animal behaviour performs as we can recognize human speech acts. Animal performances say very clearly and explicitly things like, 'Get off my territory!', 'Let's build a nest and mate', 'Give me some food', 'Take me for a walk' and so on. People are quite right to insist that by their behaviour animals say these things just as plainly and readably as people say them. True, the symbolic behaviours of, for example, seabirds engaged in courtship may need some deciphering. But the language is often easy to learn and then, as I am insisting, it is as clear as human language.

Notice, however, that these observations presuppose an intimate connection between reading a piece of behaviour, recognizing what sort of speech act it is performing, and feeling on one's own pulses its biological motivation. Human communication generally is more biologically-motivated than the older ideas about language would usually admit. A sign, we may say, is a scrap of communication, a signal, a minimum unit of social life. A word, a wink, a flash of colour, a little hint or gesture – these things are little ripples of biological feeling expressed in a bit of readable behaviour. It runs across to another, who takes the hint – and now there has been a transaction. A spark of life has been activated. We use metaphors drawn from galvanism. Life is semiotic, life is transactional, life is communication, life is publicity, display, symbolic expression. Your personality, your vitality, is your clothing, your speech, your body-language, the signals you are giving off, the messages that are emanating from you. And signs produce life, switch it on.

(ii)   Signs and the Void

Children play a game called Wordsearch. You are presented with a large grid of letters. It may be about the size of a crossword puzzle, with perhaps twelve squares in each direction. One letter is inscribed in each square, but seemingly at random, because nothing is immediately legible. You have to look for hidden words by starting from a letter and moving to its neighbour in any direction. Subsequent moves may have to continue in the same direction, or you may be allowed to twist and turn in the search for hidden meanings.

After a while you should have found a few words; but if progress is very slow you may begin to have doubts. Has the puzzle been

pre-designed at all, and in any case, how can you tell? You may
be finding words that were planted in the puzzle by a designer,
but a teacher who designs such puzzles in order to give children
practice in identifying French words tells me that children quite
often find words that were not planted. The designer lets them
slip in by mistake. And indeed it is possible that the entire puzzle
has in fact been filled in at random. If nevertheless some words
appear to you, then you are in an interesting dual position. The
meaning you perceive is in one sense truly there, but in another
sense has been dreamt up and imputed by you.

Now suppose that in a 12x12 grid you have found three or four
short words. The issue of whether the grid was pre-designed or
not hangs in the balance. But you are one of those people who
has an exceptionally strong need to seek out hidden meanings.
You get out of a pile of dictionaries and try to increase the number
of words you can find in the puzzle by drawing upon many
different languages. Does this really increase the probability that
the grid of letters has been pre-designed? I fear not. We are getting
into the position of a character in a story by J.L. Borges. The
harder we press for a solution, the more it seems to recede. The
world is becoming an endless labyrinth, and you are in danger of
becoming lost in your own obsession.[3]

To apply the analogy, the new post-realist vision of the world
portrays it as a world of signs, or (as we called it) a continuum of
language-formed events. Many of our predecessors would have
denied this, claiming that they could in one way or another
distinguish between facts and interpretations. There are bare
primary data, and there are secondary human interpretations and
inferences. For example, our sense-experiences at the first moment
of their entry upon the mental scene are innocent and purely
natural events. We cannot be deceived about them, for they are
seemings that are just what they seem. However, in recent years
we have found reason to hold that even sense-perception is already
theory-laden. When I seem to see red, I am already interpreting
what I see, for I am classifying it. I am seeing it through a word.
And unless I see through words I don't see at all. I do not have a

perspectiveless or God's-eye view of the world. On the contrary, the world is only accessible to me in so far as it is got hold of through language, interpretations, perspectives and theories. So the perceived world is indeed language-formed. In fact, the language is many layers thick.

The vision of the world as readable, as covered over with language, as a world of signs and symbols and hidden correspondences, is a typically Renaissance vision of the world.[4] But the people of the Renaissance mostly thought the code could be cracked. There was one more-or-less coherent solution to the puzzle, and when you found it you would know you had it. Today the situation is rather different. Our culture is overwhelmingly plural and abundant, globalized, and with space and time confused and disturbed. We are bombarded with an extreme excess of meanings. The delirium of our modern experience is well-reflected in our ideas about the Unconscious, and also in the recent revival of speaking with tongues.

Now, recall that the child tackling a Wordsearch had before her an array of fragments of meanings. At first, nothing seems legible. She searches around for a thread of intelligibility, a sequence that will add up to a word. She finds one, and then another. Has she fictioned these coherent sequences she has found, or were they pre-planted? Maybe there is no way to tell, and maybe it does not matter.

This example explains fictionalism. In the world about us, as in the Unconscious, we are confronted by a disorderly tumult of conflicting, multiple, fragmented meanings. Out of all this I have to select a line of sense to make. Thus, out of the excess in the Unconscious, I've got to select a thin line of clear argument. This is it. Similarly, out of the excess in the world, I've got to select a thin line of narrative to be the story of my life, the story I live by. Fictioned rationality, then, and a fictioned life-story.

One might say that in Renaissance times it looked on the whole as if the odds favoured the idea that rationality and life-story were predesigned, planted for us to trace and follow. Today, the odds rather favour the idea that we have to fiction the sense we try to speak and the lives we live. But it is hard to be sure even of that, for how could we have antecedent knowledge of what the odds either way might be expected to be?

From the principle that fiction precedes reason it is evident that philosophy only gets going *after* the initial fictioning of sentences that make sense, because philosophy must always itself make use of them. Despite the best efforts of so many of my esteemed colleagues, there is not really any nonsense-philosophy. The starting-point of philosophy has to be a chain of signs like this one, in which disorderly chaos has already been fictioned into cosmos. The disorder of the world and of the delirious Unconscious always comes first, but philosophy cannot deal with it.

This means that our doctrine of signs in what follows has to be a doctrine of them as we meet them ordered in language. Indeed, our ontology in general has to be an ontology of the world as it is continually being made sense of by language. There is no ontology of the world absolutely.

Now the sign is a material object, of sorts. It has content and form. Its content is a little flicker of biological feeling, which motivates it, makes it move. Its form is a cultural regularization of that content. Culture measures, frames, scales, differentiates, *tunes* our feeling-responses. This process gives them generality and therefore meaning. So a sign is a feeling that has been refined and shaped to become a meaning. Something common, shared.

You will not like the next step, but let us proceed. We are extremely sensitive, mutually-attuned creatures, and our regular interchanges harmonize our feelings to a very high degree. In making our feelings into general and sharable signs, culture has scaled them by various criteria. So each sign becomes a very-finely-tuned feeling which is the same for each of us.[5]

Imagine now a whole differentiated field of signs. It will be like a mosaic or a relief map. Some areas will be more salient, and others more recessed. Some will be brighter and some darker, some sweeter and some sourer, some comforting and others repulsive. Every sign will have its own very complex flavour that differentiates it from its neighbours. The whole map of signs, made up of expressed feeling-tones which our social interactions have honed and refined and made public, is the world of experience. At least, it's a people's lexicon, the order which all the time they are bringing their world into by what they say. It is a vision of the world-as-cosmos which is in constant articulation. Expressing ourselves, we are building our world.

Consider a chain of signs, a sentence. On its inner face, and with respect to its content, the sentence is an expression of feeling. Uttering it, I have given you a piece of my mind, and have got something off my chest. I feel better for that. But on its outer face the sentence connects into the public language-formed world. It is a sequence, a little thread on the field of signs, something imposed or found, I am not sure which – just as the schoolgirl found a thread of intelligibility on her Wordsearch grid of letters. In Wordsearch the custom is to draw an oval cartouche in outline around the word that you have found or made. Rather similarly, when I make some kind of factual assertion about the things in front of me, I am so to say singling out an intelligible sequence from the extremely complex verbal fuzz around. I have picked out a sentence, made it or found it. I have imposed order upon a little bit of the world.

Two complications or qualifications. First, my subjectivity, remember, is not something special or privileged that stands right out of the field of signs. On the contrary, I am out in front. I am in the field of signs, part of it. A human being is as it were an area culturally-trained to generate sentences around itself. We are impelled to try to get at least our own environs into some kind of linguistic order. But to keep ahead of chaos one has to talk fast. Articulacy is the capacity to impose and maintain some degree of order around one.

The second complication. Signs in a chain are not atomic and don't function independently. In this matter our thinking about signs has developed pretty much as our thinking about genes has developed. In each case the part functions in and through a whole system. Signs as it were overlap heavily. Each sign gives something to earlier ones further back down the line, and also borrows a bit from them; while at the same time it must wait itself to be clarified by what comes after. The sign acts within a successively-unfolding series, and the precise job it does is not fully crystallized until it is long gone.

All this is very familiar in the interpretation of prose text, but it is equally true of other and seeming more solitary signs. A speed-limit sign, for example, may look as if it stands alone with its meaning contained in itself. But in fact it is like a word in that its significance for you will vary very greatly according to the narrative context in which you meet it. You may see the sign while you are driving at a higher speed than it specifies and with a police car behind you. You may see it resting in a Highways Department store. You may see it misappropriated and fixed on the wall of some high-spirited student's room. You may see it while you are walking or cycling. In these different situations its meaning for you will be very different. And in general, a sign, which in a dictionary or Highway Code seems to be portrayed as being stiff and self-enclosed, in fact needs a narrative context to activate it and give it a specific force. Different narrative contexts may activate the same sign in a surprising variety of different ways, just as the force of a particular word-use depends on the language-game within which it occurs.

Because sentences are temporally-extended, because meaning is highly contextual and depends upon what the story is, and because therefore a word's meaning depends *both* upon much that is already said and done and gone *and* upon much that is yet to be made clear, there is no point in the sequence at which the sign's whole meaning is clear, fully-given and present. Meaning as such is radically temporal and processual. It is always transient, always both coming to be and passing away, always both appearing and disappearing, and never fully mastered.

That is what I mean by the Void. The Void is opened by the insubstantiality, the relativity, the transience and the lack of any hard centre in the sign itself. The Void is not an empty space between solid signs. The Void is universal slipping-away, central to and constitutive of everything.

Yet the Void in this sense is what actually makes life and meaning possible. The Void is just movement, change. Semeiosis, signification, is a temporal moving process. Philosophy in its heyday always found this very difficult to accept. But, *contra* Plato, it now seems that interrelatedness, difference, succession and insubstantiality are conditions of intelligibility. Just reading a sentence, we should be able to feel on our pulses the way life and meaning continually come out of the Void and return into it.

That's the new religious object. *That's* what we have to learn to say yes to. *That's* what the end of realism obliges us to confront. If you like, the necessity of ephemerality, life's urgent transience.

(iii)   Co-humanity

Meaning is entirely publicly-established, and syntax is compulsory. This means that private individual selfhood is derivative. We need therefore to modify our notion of individual freedom, rather as earlier we suggested that the notion of individual self-consciousness needs to be modified. Attributes just of the individual cannot now be given quite the foundational significance they have sometimes had in the past. Both consciousness and freedom need as it were to be publicized; that is, we need to think them through the way they are exercised in the public domain. This will mean that we will not think of them as so to say attached to individuals. For the truth is that everything important happens along the wires and in the space between people. The human is inter-subjectivity, co-humanity. It is the general field of discourse, humming with transactions. This public realm can almost be thought of as a living, changing organism. A venerable metaphor sees individuals as being like cells in its body. So we might with advantage think of freedom and consciousness not so much as individual powers, but rather as being adverbial qualities of the continuing public debate – its level, the range of contributions being made to it, its degree of self-criticism and so forth. Freedom

and self-consciousness, I shall suggest, are enjoyed by participation.

Now let's take some of these ideas by stages. Like market prices,
the meanings of words are produced and sustained by daily
transactions in the public realm. Meaning is not so much use
as usage. It is something current, like reputation or standing,
something that we have to speak of as being 'kept up', and as
being always fluctuating. Meaning, then, is public and processual;
yet we are entirely dependent upon its current state for our ability
to think even our most private thoughts. The current public world
motorways through our heads. You cannot keep it out, and you
cannot let anything else in. If you doubt this, then try to invent a
new meaning and then see if you can find a way to domesticate it
so that it will run along and mingle freely with other words in
your spontaneously moving trains of thought. Go on: try. You
find however that it is impossible. The interloper simply cannot
get itself accepted. Living and socially-produced meanings are
the only meanings there are, and I cannot insert an artificially
manufactured one among them.

How then can meaning-change ever be initiated? We should
consider here how an outstandingly fertile inventor of new
metaphors, such as Freud, goes about it. He makes the most of
such latitude as the language permits him. He sets out to establish
new connections, coin new metaphors, revive archaisms, stretch
existing uses a little, and exploit puns, ambiguities and equivoci-
ties. A creative person makes the most of whatever loopholes
there may be in the language, very much as a chartered accountant
looks for loopholes in the tax laws.

Interestingly, even when one does succeed in adding a new
metaphorical twist to an established pattern of usage, it still
cannot be directly taken into one's own spontaneous thinking. It
first has to be given a little public currency. That is why people
write and publish – in order to assimilate their own thinking.
When I have a new idea, it is at first as alien, repellent and obscure
to me as it is to people in general. I can do little with it. It has to
be expressed, articulated, published, circulated, and then quietly

remain current for two or three years. There may be very little evidence that anybody is using it or taking any notice of it, yet somehow a few years of exposure to the open air seems to take off its rough edges, smoothe it, tame it and make it easier to assimilate. Thus by a striking paradox I can only fully get hold of my own ideas by getting rid of them. Only in the public realm can meanings become clarified, because only in the public realm can they learn to settle down amongst other meanings, find their place and fit in. I am so dependent upon the public realm that I can only take in my own thinking after a detour through it.

Similarly considerations apply – but even more strongly – to syntax. Such private thoughts as any of us may have are constrained by publicly-established syntactical structures. We cannot step out of them at will. For example, after studying the (written) Chinese language awhile, I may decide that Western grammar and syntax are too substance-oriented and therefore too reifying. They make us think that there is a real difference between nouns and verbs, what things are and what they do. We want there to be nouns-out-there, stable topics of discourse that keep a firm hold on their identity. But the result has been that Western thought has always had difficulty in thinking time, change, activity and the flow of life. Even though language itself is temporal, I still find it hard to think in sequences. I find sculpture easier to appreciate than ballet, and prefer paintings to the cinema. I would like to be able to think more consistently temporally, so I look at Chinese with interest. In it, sentences express forces. The language runs along with the way biological feeling flows and discharges, and with the way life runs and expends itself in time. I'd like to be able to think Chinese, and so perhaps understand East Asian Buddhism better. But can I do it? Of course I can't. I can only think Western. I would only be able spontaneously to think Chinese if I were immersed in China for many years without functioning at all in any other language, and that would make me into someone else.

If then meaning is entirely publicly-established and syntax is compulsory, and if I cannot step right outside my own culture and period, then I am obliged to acknowledge that my individual selfhood is a cultural product. I can in various ways enlarge the house of culture, for I can push back its walls and incorporate into it perspectival views of any and all other places and times. But I am not actually free to step out of the house altogether. I cannot become an eighteenth-century person or a Peruvian. Culture is the living moving public cultural sign-system. It is language plus all its offshoots in the way of art, ritual, customs and the rest. We swim in it like fish in water. It forms our feelings, our ideas about gender, our values and our style of selfhood. And it permits us a range, but only a limited range, of sorts of persons that we can become.

Culturalism, the realization of the primacy and ubiquity of culture, is very recent. The three main factors in forming it have been French social theory since Durkheim and Lévy-Bruhl, the population movements which have now made so many of the Western democratic countries multi-cultural, and the role of the mass media in making it easy for us to look in upon other people's worlds. But all these factors have come fully into operation only in the period since the 1950s, and the term 'culturalism' has come into use still more recently.[6] It hasn't yet settled down, but it is already beginning to have a disturbing effect upon its neighbours – and especially upon its antonym, naturalism. It is splitting naturalism apart, confirming one meaning of it but terminating and replacing another.

To see why, we must distinguish two different senses of naturalism. One lives, the other is dying. According to the first, naturalism defines itself by its opposition to supernaturalism and to any sort of metaphysics of transcendence. Naturalism repudiates any kind of appeal to invisible spirits, standards or powers. It wants to bring everything down to one level, and to make everything part of one and the same regular unfolding horizontal process. Naturalism does not want even the human mind or 'absolute' moral standards to be exempt from this generalization. All explanations and predictions have to be in terms of recurrent patterns and other design-features on a flat unrolling tapestry. In fact, only horizontal explanation is explanation at all; explanation from above is a lie and a deception.[7]

Here, naturalism and culturalism are in agreement. Culturalism too is one-level, immanent and continuous in outlook. It too rejects traditional metaphysical ideas of noumenal reality, spiritual substance and so forth. One might perhaps situate Hegel's philosophy in the area where naturalism and culturalism overlap without quarrelling. There are also various forms of religious and ethical naturalism which can just as well be called culturalist.

However, in another and second sense naturalism is the opposite of culturalism. For naturalism may be understood as trying to bring everything down to Nature. Here, the natural is defined as that which is precisely *not* human, 'positive;' and socially-instituted. Nature is seen as a real cosmic order out there, the setting of human life, a world of fact prior to and independent of our human interpretations. It is a law-abiding physical world, a world of material events, particles, forces or sensibilia. We have evolved out of it and all our cultural products are in the end answerable back to it. It is that against which all our theories have to be tested. Culture must bow to Nature.

Naturalism in this latter sense is hard-nosed scientific realism or materialism, as represented in Britain at present by, for example, P.W. Atkins and Richard Dawkins.[8] Yet it is a puzzling and strangely unreflective doctrine, for it requires Atkins and Dawkins to be unaware of language even as they use it, and to represent as an abiding extra-cultural reality a vision of the cosmos that has taken shape only *within* Western culture during recent generations. They are using a cultural product to undercut Culture. In short, the difficulty we now have in understanding scientific realism is the same as our difficulty in understanding theological realism. Why do people still want to think in these enslaved and mythical ways, and how do they manage it? In both cases an act of repression or self-obfuscation has been carried out. Realists trick themselves into projecting out their fictions by concealing from themselves the currency in which they are trading. So scientists, even good scientists, can write a book without ever once noticing that the book is in *writing*. The text then becomes for them invisible, a clear window upon natural reality. The reader seems to look straight through the text at an objective world. The cultural has repressed itself into seeming transparency.

But that is how culture always used to work, in the old days before we had the concept of culture. The cultural realm hid itself form itself, in order to create a hierarchized and objective reality. Before the new awareness of culture developed, we distinguished between natural and supernatural, *Natur* and *Geist*, the phenomenal and noumenal, fact and interpretation, the actual and the ideal, and so on. We made a great many of these realistic distinctions. But I am saying that the distinctions have all broken down. To replace them we need a new distinction, one between culture and reflection. For culturalism is of course anti-realist, *and knows it*. That is to say, culturalism knows that the world is only an endlessly shifting purely contingent order of signs in motion, a Sea of Meanings. Within it are produced narratives, world-views, desires and forms of selfhood, all of them fleeting. And just the ability to see this and say it is precisely what gives us our new and joyful freedom. For in our late twentieth-century world culture's new and very intense awareness of itself creates a vivid ironical self-reflexivity. Culture knows that is only culture, myth that it is only myth, religious faith that its object is internal to it. Your God is only your faith in him, your values are only your commitment to them. That is liberation. You're free.

Strangely, primitive thought was correct: reality can only be conferred from outside. A thing was made real in so far as it participated virtually in some mythic Archetype.[9] But our culturalist and postmodern world is radically outsideless. It therefore does not get itself made real from outside. It remains a mere fashion and a fiction that we sustain, a tenuous shifting thing. But because it knows this, it is very highly reflective, and its ironical awareness of its own contingency and 'unreality' makes it very easily changeable. So there is no shortage of freedom and consciousness now. True, I don't have the pure metaphysical consciousness and freedom of the old philosophy of subjectivity, because I am not that two-level kind of being. I am not a Cartesian subject, and I don't suppose that philosophy can be founded on the inference 'I think, therefore I am'. But because we all participate in the movement of the public world of signs, we participate in and contribute to the general self-reflexive consciousness of modern culture and to the process of social change. The essential idea is that in our new situation both self-consciousness and freedom of action have become participatory.

Sure, there's a political problem: under late capitalism a few individual magnates buy up publications and broadcasting organizations. They are trying to gain control of the means of communication. And they are indeed disproportionately articulate. But there is a political remedy, too. Those who are not getting a fair hearing need to be given more access. We should strive to help the dumb to speak.

(iv)   The body of signs

The human body is the great unknown of Western thought, denied and forgotten since early times.[10] During antiquity, in the Greco-Roman world, 'the flesh' gradually came to be associated with shame, weakness, temptation, corruptibility, suffering and death. The blight had begun to settle even before the rise of Christianity, and is still not fully lifted. And the reason for it is not hard to find.[11] It is through the body that we are selves, woven into the fabric of the empirical world, so that whatever may be wrong with the world at large must be wrong also with the body in particular. But around the time of Plato and the Buddha, a certain world-pessimism descended upon India, Greece and other places. Philosophy and religion began to seek blessedness by escaping from the world – and therefore also from the body. This in turn meant that an immortal real Self had to be posited, and dissociated from the body.

This split between an invisible core-self and one's social bodily self is a very awkward one to make. How do you do it? Just consider how in the Narcissus story and elsewhere, self-image is body-image. We look at our *selves* in the mirror, not at something else. Consider too how the term 'person' is still in many idioms used to mean the body. But as our persons came to seem no longer personable to us, it was thought necessary to deny that a person co-incides with his or her bodily person. So the real Self gradually ceased to be the bodily-presented self in the social relationships of this life, and became instead an inward and hidden spiritual substance, the soul.[12] Its self-consciousness and self-identity were increasingly thought of as realised independently of the body. It was constituted by its own participation in Eternal Reason, or by its relation to God. It regarded the body as little more than an external envelope and an embarrassing – but only temporary – companion, and it saw human relationships in this world as a distraction or even a threat. And since language shares many or all of the faults of the world and the body, it too needed to be repudiated. Accordingly it came to be supposed that the soul's characteristic activity, thought, was a non-linguistic and purely spiritual operation, something you could go on doing after you had become disembodied. 'Thought' ideally involved something like telepathic communication, spiritual apprehension and intuitive vision. The metaphors seem to credit the soul with a ghostly mouth, hands and eyes.

The newly-fabricated inner self, the immortal rational soul, exercised its wings especially in pure thought, in philosophical contemplation and in prayer. Think what prayer involved and still involves: you became physically motionless, you sought out a quiet place and closed your eyes (so reducing the input of sensory information), and you sought generally to calm the passions, slow the self down, and turn within. Thus in every possible way you distanced yourself from the volatile noisy gregariousness of the body and society. The very symbolism of prayer implies a deep mistrust of the external world.

In such a context it is not surprising that after Plato the study of the human self gradually became less a study of people's visible and social self-expression, and more an investigation of the inner

68

space of the soul. The self was to be accessed by introspection. New metaphors and new discourses were required in order to describe what was happening within the postulated inner space of the psyche. The first and most popular of the new metaphors described psychic life in terms of an interplay or struggle between opposed voices or forces. I have in mind here the discourses of asceticism and the struggle for self-mastery, allegory, spirituality, thought-processes and psychology. And my argument is that the more elaborated these discourses became, the more deeply the body slipped into obscurity and was forgotten. All talk of selfhood became talk about things happening in the fictioned inner theatre of psychic conflict and mental activities. The body was displaced, pushed out of sight.

To this day many people fail to appreciate how very odd all of this is. But consider: we still have and make extensive use of a large vocabulary to describe events in the mental-spiritual-psychological realm. This vocabulary uses ponderous physical metaphors to conjure up a picture of what is happening in an inner space – which is supposedly not 'literally' bodily, or spatial, or inside us at all. And this non-bodily inner space was originally opened up by way of helping us to distance ourselves from our own bodies.

Am I making the absurdity of all this plain? We fled from the body and worldly sociability and tried to locate the real core-Self in a non-bodily and even non-linguistic private inner space seen only by God. But to make the goings-on in this special inner space of subjectivity accessible, we had to invent a whole lot of new bodily metaphors. So as soon as the bodily had been pushed out of the front door, it had to be let in again at the back. And what a lot we did let in! The inner life of the self was described as like what happens in a theatre or courthouse, or on a battlefield. It involved struggles, conflicts, fierce debates and arduous athletic exercises. It involved the processing and the filing of a great deal of information, and much heavy clanking of machinery. Nobody does all this more egregiously than Freud himself. He stuffs us with inner machinery, and my complaint is that by so greatly elaborating the dubious physical metaphors of our supposedly non-physical psychic life, Freud makes confusion worse confounded. The body is becoming more lost than ever.

It is time to cut the knot. Let us abolish the mind and all its works. Instead, we begin with a very simple metaphor – which is a bit more than a metaphor. Inside me, beneath my skin surface, I am just an animal, and you will find nothing there but squishy biology. Everything that makes me human is on the surface, where you will find an immense amount of cultural activity taking place. I am clothed, moving around, expressing myself. My surfaces quiver with varied sense-experiences, visual, auditory, tactile and so on. My whole aspect is in various ways labelled and structured by culture. Just to begin with, the body has various culturally-inscribed permissions and prohibitions written on it, so that there are bits of it that can touch others and be touched by them, bits that are displayed in public, naughty bits and so on. So there are cultural rules inscribed upon the surface, and also a great many signs in motion across the surface. Like Ray Bradbury's *Illustrated Man*,[13] we receive and give off a continual stream of stories and messages through our dress, grooming, body-language, gait, manner, signature, speech, self-presentation, visible feeling-responses and so on.

So we define the real human social self as the body surface, which is a vestment of cultural signs. Some are like fixed inscriptions, and others are in rapid movement. This living shirt of meanings, this coat of many colours, has biological desire filling it out on the inside, and it has the atmospheric pressure, as it were, of external reality bearing down upon it from the outside. The two pressures balance each other. The shirt is a frontier or interface. On it, culture produces us and we participate in culture. The sign evokes desire, and desire moves the sign.

Now, we are *homo sapiens*, that is, we are the species that exists only as a cultural being with a shirt on. An animal is just an animal, but with us even a nude is still fully shirted. That is, the nude is not animal, but remains cultural. It positively bristles with cultural meanings. The line 'Love is the living shirt of flame' suggests to me that it is the movement of cultural signs on our surface which continually activates and energizes our biological life. That is why the socially-presented and visible person *is* the body and *is* the real self. I am my outer surface, and my outer surface, my persona is my body. The apparent is the real. A legible body, a body of signs, a human and culturally-formed body.

The whole self would be the whole body, fully read. But it never is so, of course. The self others know is their interpretation or reading of the body's appearances to them. So I am what you make of me. It is because selfhood is a show and a performance, and because we read each other's appearances, that such arts as the cinema and the theatre are possible *at all*. If the real self were something hidden, and accessible only to itself and to God, then we would not have the data to make well-founded judgments about the characters in a film and the morality of their behaviour. But happily the self is just appearance. It is the presented self, the personality, the legible self; and psychology, at least on the everyday level, is an interpretative, literary sort of subject.

It is certainly possible for my own account of myself to be in various ways defective or incomplete. This may become apparent, as when there is a manifest discrepancy between the story I am telling you and what is suggested by my body-language. Such visible incongruity may be quite sufficient to justify talk about lies, hypocrisy, pretence or self-deception, as may be appropriate in a particular instance. There is no need at this point to invoke the traditional contrast between deceptive outward appearance and deep inner truth. We don't have to think of reinstating the appearance-reality distinction, which in any case is not very helpful. We do better to go by the excellent idiom which says that people may 'send out conflicting signals'. Quite right; they often do.

What of the contrast which we mentioned, between fixed inscriptions and moving signs? To develop this idea, compare the body-surface with a playing-field. Next, make a distinction between the way the field is marked out for play, and the play that takes place on the field. A field with boundaries, goals,

penalty-zones and so marked out upon it is a field prepared for
the playing of a particular game such as hockey. Similarly, the
relatively fixed inscriptions upon the human body structure it for
the playing of a certain social role. One's gender identity is the
obvious example. We may feel dissatisfied with the way what it
is to be a man and what it is to be a woman are presently defined
in our society. We may feel that the pattern of some fixed
inscription ought to be drawn in a different way, but it is only
prudent to remind ourselves that the markings are, as people say,
engrained. Over the generations they do come to get drawn in
different ways and places. But anyone who tries to shift them in
a hurry will meet resistance.

Some utopians have dreamt of a society without any distinctions
of gender, class, nationality and the like. But the game metaphor
suggests that this may be impossible. Why? Consider this series
of propositions. There is no human life without a movement of
signs. There is no movement of signs except in some form of
symbolic *exchange*. But exchange has to follow rules, which
constitute it as a play of differences. And if all this is correct, then
ritual is a permanent feature of human life. Social life just consists
in a ding-dong of rule-governed symbolic exchange between
complementary opposites, as in a competitive team game, or as
in the perennial wars between woman and man, or teacher and
pupil. If so, there will always be fixed inscriptions and role-play.
Some periods are obviously more relaxed and informal than
others; but that ritual should ever be wholly abandoned is scarcely
imaginable.

(v) The regime of the sign

When someone comes into the room or simply appears before us,
communication is opened at once. It has to be; it cannot not be. I
may complain that she treated me as if I wasn't there, as if I did
not exist. I mean by this that she failed to respond in any way to
my signals: she affected to disregard me. But this affectation of

disregard is itself something evident. Even the put-down or negative communication is still a communication, and I've got the message all right.

It's bad news. For the example suggests that when two people are in each other's presence at all then they are in communication, and conversely that the end of all communication is a state of banishment or exile in which one is out of sight and out of mind. We are dead to each other, and it is as if I am buried alive. All the idioms compare being incommunicado with a state of death. Ordinarily we keep *in touch*, a phrase which vividly suggests the equivalence of presence, contact and communication.

There is a period before the age of two-and-a-half or so when young children will play in the same room quite oblivious of each other. This behaviour strikes older people as odd, because we who have been fully inducted into language are under the regime of the sign. That is, for us communication is compulsory. We exist in our relationships, and the need for recognition by others and accord with them precedes all else.

Our communicativeness means that we are always something to each other. Many or even perhaps most human relationships are marked by inequality of power, but despite what people may say no relationship can become quite one-sided. Even the most dominant person still needs the other to be audience or victim; even the most passive and submissive character remains something to the other. The communicational relationship precedes the inequality of power.

The regime of culture then is a regime of communication. As we have seen, it involves fixed inscriptions that assign our basic roles to us, ritual exchanges within a great variety of game-situations, and an order of signs in which to conduct these exchanges. Within this very highly conventionalized regime we live. But how, how did this regime of culture first get established, and what legitimates it and maintains it? What *is* culture, what is its power, and how did it begin? We need a theory of how cultural inscriptions got branded upon us, and also some account of what sort and measure of freedom there is still left to us. Most of the historic discussions of freedom try to give an account of it *vis-à-vis* the power and wisdom of God, *vis-à-vis* physical necessity, or *vis-à-vis* political authority. Debate about the ways in which language and culture frame and limit our freedom does not have such a long history. But if we take a contemporary case such as the comparative freedom of young women members of Asian, Muslim and Western communities, it seems clear that culture is the single most important constraint upon freedom. Culture defines what kind of freedom is going to be permitted to us, and what measure of it we are going to get. Culture lays down the terms.

There is a further consideration: as we have seen, the modern debate about language-games, role-play, 'situations'[14] and so forth makes us realize that human conversation is ritualized. There is always a game-situation which prescribes what sort of things can be said, and how what the other may say is to be taken. I have been suggesting that in all our relationships there is some sort of ritual conflict. That is, there is a rule-governed to-and-fro of symbolic exchange between complementary opposites, or at least a play of differences. Hence all those metaphors about battles of wits and verbal fencing or sparring. Some sort of trading, conflict or batting back and forth in a language-game is always going on. That is why people go to watch a tennis match, or any other kind of gladiatorial combat: it is an allegory or a dramatization of our ordinary human relations. But this makes it clear that the daily business of life is much more ritualized than the older thinkers admitted. What then of freedom?

Let us first raise the question of why ritualized communication, little verbal games, trials of wit and power struggles should be so necessary to us. In section (*i*) above I argued that animal communication can be recognized as such by its biological motivation. It has developed because it benefits the communicator. A bit of animal behaviour is a communication if it influences the behaviour of another animal in a way that is the former's advantage. The behaviour has evolved because there is a pay-off in terms of survival to reproduce. For example, it helps to get the animal a mate or a meal. Notice too that in this animal case ritualization equals readability: the advantageous behaviour will not evolve unless it and the other animal's response to it are the same each time.

In our own case the fundamental condition for our survival is agreement. We have got to be on net, part of the human cultural communications network. When we get right out of touch, we are cold and dead. Many people regard the regime of culture as being needlessly oppressive, and suspect in it some sort of conspiracy – of men against women, of the old against the young, of the strong against the weak, of the priesthood against the laity, or whatever. Such factors may, I suppose, have influenced the way culture has developed; but the biological parallels with the communicative behaviour of other social animals suggest that the overriding consideration is our need to establish and maintain consent, mutual understanding and co-operation. Consider the behaviour by which a pair of seabirds form and strengthen the bond between them. So it is with us: constant daily signalling back and forth keeps us all on net. Our behaviours become reciprocally adapted, harmonized and interwoven in a way that is to the advantage of each.

On this account, there is no sharp distinction between culture and nature. Human beings are simply the animals for whom cultural life is a biological necessity. The pressure of culture's regime upon us is not merely a pressure of the strong upon the weak, or of men upon women. If it were only that, it might be thrown off – and it cannot be. For the pressure of culture is a pressure which we all of us continually exert upon each other. It is a reciprocal clamour for attention and demand for conformity. It is rather like what eighteenth-century moralists used to call 'the popular sanction', the pressure of public opinion upon our behaviour. Its outcome is the whole system of signs and the valuations annexed to them; a very large field of agreed-upon, mutually-adjusted and generally-recognized little behaviours and responses thereto. We can exert pressure either positively by the dominance behaviour that seeks to compel agreement, or negatively by the submissive behaviour that readily yields and concedes it. Either way, the goal is the establishment and maintenance of the whole system of inter-related, balanced micro-behaviours that we call a natural language. The force that keeps the whole thing pumped up and in place, relatively stable, is everyone's fear of isolation and death, and therefore everyone's attention-seeking and pressurizing behaviour.

There are various degrees of strictness of the cultural regime. When a society is swept by an epidemic of fear or a moral panic, there is a sudden horror that the whole system of cultural controls upon behaviour may become disordered or contaminated, or may break down altogether. The result is a popular demand for a stricter regime. It is noteworthy that the people who ask for stricter moral discipline and tighter control of potentially disorderly forces such as art and sex are also the semantic and grammatical precisionists. People evidently feel that there is a very close affinity between linguistic and moral laxity.

A continual see-saw between the principles of order and freedom, strictness and laxity, conservative and liberal has, since the later seventeenth century, become a feature of the life of all large-scale modern societies. It seems that as the culture becomes more urbanized and highly differentiated, with an ever wider range of different ways of life open to us, we sense more possibilities of freedom. We see that culture changes, that social controls can relax, and that we might be able to get away with it – but now there is a flicker of fear. The greater freedom and anonymity of city life brings with it also a sense of alienation. I find I am in a love-hate relationship to the old social controls: they held me close, but at least they made me somebody. In the ampler and more complex cultural world of someone making their way in a modern city we begin to fear that the individual no longer understands the whole and no longer has a personal stake in it. So there are complaints about feeling lost, and there is nostalgia for the small-scale, face-to-face social world of the village.

If we thus yearn both for freedom and for order, it is not surprising that since the Romantic Movement and the philosophy of Hegel so many people have dreamt of a fresh synthesis of the two. A society so cunningly planned that the whole economic system is driven by the individual's restless search for personal happiness and fulfilment: a consumer society. This is a type of society which has its own highly distinctive regime of signs, which works as a complex machine for producing, forming and gratifying individual dreams and wishes, and which raises interesting questions about personal freedom.

In late-capitalist society the most powerful cultural forces are the media, advertising, logos, brand names and above all the consumer product. The concept of a product has recently widened to include everything that is designed for a market. So there are now financial products such as investment plans, credit facilities and personal pensions. There are holiday and travel packages, cars and restaurant meals. Increasingly, education, culture, entertainment and health also become marketed products. And there is in addition the vast array of what are called 'goods' in the shops.

In postmodern times it is as if the whole of society has become a marketplace. The market is highly segmented into niches, and elaborately scaled with many rungs up and down the ladder. Everything in the entire system of product ranges, scaled vertically and segmented laterally, is wrapped up in a highly attractive packaging of signs and energetically publicized in the marketplace. So vast and so seductive is the resulting display that for many city dwellers 'the bright lights' – all the signs surrounding goods and products of every kind – almost coincides with the world of experience as described in section (ii). Its ordered array is the new class system. It symbolizes and forms the social order.[15] You used to belong to a class, but now you have a level or slot in the market, tailored and all ready for you to drop into it.

Computer control of mass-production systems has recently greatly enhanced the extent to which the product can be customized or personalized to suit your individual taste. The car manufacturer can easily supply any one of a very large number of possible combinations of model, colour and extras. So it is also with many other products, too. Everything's laid on. You are what the system has prepared for you to buy. Buying, you fit into your predestined niche, fulfil your personal dream, and do your economic duty as a consumer. Thus the late-capitalist economy promises the most perfect synthesis of total social organization and total personal fulfilment yet achieved on earth. It is very like the medieval Heaven, but is less moralistic, pernickety and disapproving than religion used to be. It personalizes the gratification it gives you, gives it without any hint of reproach, and gives it to you here and now, in this life. When you shop, pure self-indulgence and the performance of your social duty are one and the same. What religion used to call faith is now rechristened consumer confidence. And the system is matchlessly thorough in the way it uses advertising to arouse and direct our desires, market research to measure them and design and technology to gratify them.

Everything hangs together, in this new society of ours. The whole system manifests a most extraordinarily potent synthesis of the principles of order and freedom, self-indulgence and social control. And it is still improving and becoming more efficient. At the ideal limit, when you purchase a consumer product you will be doing four things simultaneously and they will all exactly coincide. You will be doing what the system has preprogrammed you to do, you will be exercising your right of free choice in an open market, you will be doing your moral duty as an economically active citizen, and you will be purely indulging yourself.

This synthesis is not an original idea. On the contrary, it is derived straight from Western theology, which from Augustine to Leibniz had dreamt of exactly this synthesis of divine predestination and human freedom, duty and inclination. They reserved it for heaven and priced the entry ticket high, whereas we are achieving it on earth; but the synthesis is the same. It is an order in which to serve is to reign, and in which our duty is our heart's desire. And it is all brought about by the rich and highly-managed sign-regime that we have nowadays, the regime of advertising, the media and design, which has so pervasively aestheticized life.

People's subjection to this regime appears to be entirely voluntary. The average British family is reported to watch television for five hours a day – and that is before they have started in on newspapers, magazines, radio, pop music and the cinema, not to mention the time spent in shopping. The system works, by heaven it works. Nobody will vote against having a part in it. When the citizens of the old GDR crossed the border into West Berlin, they were like Victorian ragamuffins with their noses pressed against the shop windowpanes. They promptly forgot the New Forum politicians and voted for consumerism – as everyone would.

It is not easy to get any critical leverage against late capitalism. Those who call it materialistic – confident, somehow, that that is a serious charge – forget that by its elegant synthesis of order and freedom, duty and desire, it has largely fulfilled the dream of Western Christian thought at least from Augustine to Hegel. If this is crass materialism, well, it is what our tradition sought;[16] and if the way the system works still excludes a substantial slice of the population, the same was true in the past. We have our underclass, they had their Hell. The difference is that there is no reason in principle why we should not in time empty the underclass, whereas Hell was a permanent and irremediable condition.

Nor is it easy to criticize the system for being manipulative, when people so readily collaborate in their own manipulation. They are eager to devise advertising slogans, answer market researchers' questions and enter promotional competitions. And if the world of language and culture really is outsideless, then there is no independent nature of things or standpoint outside the system from which it can be criticized. Within the system people are genuinely getting what the system makes them genuinely desire, and what's wrong with that? Nobody has access to an extra-cultural and purely independent standard by which to determine what is 'really' to be desired by human beings, and what 'really' should satisfy their desires. There is no superior or 'natural' reality by contrast with which the world of late capitalism is mere appearance. I cannot usefully condemn it as frothy if there is nothing but froth. Besides, this book is a consumer product too; the point being that any argument or artwork that tries to criticize our present cultural system must itself be packaged as a commodity and traded within the system. Jean Baudrillard, whose very pessimistic criticisms of late capitalism have been so influential during the past decade or two, seems not to notice this reflexive difficulty with his own argument.

It is important not to be paranoid. There are some reasons for holding that our present cultural regime is comparatively very lax. I cite four.

First, we enjoy the advantage of having at last shaken off the old penal-moralistic type of cosmology that dominated much of humanity until quite recently.[17] Remember, it was almost universally believed that there was objectively only one true and unchanging morality, and that the Universe was so constructed as to instil and enforce it minutely. Moral realism, a moral world-order, a moral Providence, a Last Judgment, Heaven and Hell: these were fearful ideas. You lived your entire life under a police caution. Everything you thought, said and did was being written down and would on the Last Day be cited against you. What I have been calling culture's (relatively) fixed inscriptions on our skin surface was in those days an eternal Divine Law written on our hearts. The very same Law ruled the church, the state and even the whole cosmos, and would in the end prevail absolutely. By contrast with that cosmic terrorism, our present world is nothing like so strictly policed. If we don't like our present cultural inscriptions and moral values, we have the great comfort of knowing that they are not absolutes and they can be changed. We, we can do it.

Secondly, in bourgeois society the communication codes become partly deritualized. Formal dress tends to be replaced by casual wear, and social relations similarly become more informal and improvised. Maybe the loss of many of the old rituals, manners and conventions brings its own problems, but that is a separate argument. The present claim is merely that despite what is said by pessimists such as Foucault and Baudrillard, there are many obvious respects in which social controls are a bit less strict than they were and we have a little more freedom to make up our own lives.

Thirdly, we now have access to an unprecedented abundance of different occupations, consumer goods, cultural resources and communication channels. Following Foucault, the pessimists see in this increasing differentiation the development of an ever-more-minute regulation of life. But the optimists, with more plausibility, can reply that if a house has got far more rooms in it than you'll ever be able to explore in all your life, you cannot reasonably complain that it's a prison.

Fourthly, we argued in section (*iii*) that in the age of the sign consciousness and freedom need to be theorized in terms of the way they are exercised in the public domain. That means: people remain free in so far as we can demonstrate that new words and new usages are still being coined and adopted, and the value-flavours annexed to words are being changed. But this process, so far as we can tell, is happening more rapidly now than ever before. The rate of social change is the best evidence of our freedom. While time goes on we can keep on becoming reflexively conscious of the system, and innovating.

This review suggests that the optimists have on the whole the better of the argument. It also suggests a more important conclusion, namely that closure is the enemy of freedom and time the friend. Following our best religious and philosophical tradition, our present late capitalist culture strives for a perfect synthesis of order and freedom, duty and inclination. If it were ever to achieve the total consumer satisfaction that it aims for, then it would indeed make slaves of us. Fortunately, the effort is being made in time, and therefore finalization or 'closure' cannot be reached. The sign moves on. Language, interpretation and revaluation continue End-lessly. Eternity would put an end to freedom and quench the spirit.

We need – don't we know it by now? – a religion without God, that is, a religion without absolutes, without perfection, without closure, without eternity. A religion of creativity and freedom must be a religion that says yes to time, contingency, open-endedness, transience. We have always pictured time as a destroyer; but it is also the redeemer.

6

WHAT IS WRONG WITH US

(i) Tragedy is cultural

Schopenhauer says somewhere that man is a squirrel in a cage. This image suggests that our human condition is so-to-say objectively or cosmically tragic. We know we could be free and leaping though the trees, but we find ourselves hemmed in by fixed and immovable limitations. So there is a straight conflict between a permanent natural fact about us and a permanent natural fact about our circumstances. The conflict cannot be overcome, and that is our tragedy.

It is clear that Schopenhauer's doctrine about the human condition and how tragic it is can only get off the ground if some vital doctrines of naturalism are true. First, there's got to be a structured, extra-cultural nature of things, both out there in the world and inside us humans. Secondly, philosophy has got to be able to investigate this objective nature of things and spell out what it's like in a lot of very general sentences. Thirdly, the statements of this philosophical anthropology have got to be universal truths that have the same force and the same value for everyone in all possible human cultural worlds.

That makes it clear that Schopenhauer is wrong. There is no Truth of the human condition as such. There is no completely extra-cultural, extra-historical vocabulary in which universal truths about human nature and the human condition could be formulated. When I study Western writers, such as Augustine, Luther, Kierkegaard and Heidegger, I am studying a literary tradition. These writers did not look at something out there called the human condition, and then make up descriptive sentences about it. What happened was that each of them first read his predecessors, and then added a new text continuing their tradition. In this way all images of what a human being is, what our life is, and what the ambient limits of our condition are – all such images are literary artefacts worked up within literary traditions.

I am a Westerner, God help me, so my inner life is like an Ingmar Bergman film, for the very good reason that the films and I are artefacts produced within one and the same cultural tradition. As a result, you, I and the films all have the same problems – original sin, concupiscence, the old Adam (or the old Eve, as the case may be), a malcontent subjectivity, the bondage of the will, dread, the need for grace and so on. But all this stuff is culture, not nature. When I take up Buddhist writings I enter a very different cultural world, in which over the centuries human nature and the human condition came to be constructed quite otherwise. As a result many of our hang-ups have not troubled them at all, and it is a great relief to learn this. I come to take a non-realist view of my own squirrel-cage, when I see that it is only a Western cultural artefact. True, it still holds me for the present. But the study of other cultural constructions of the self and the human condition encourages the thought that, given time, we may be able to redesign our own condition and make it more comfortable and less constricting.

There is, then, no human nature as such, and no set of rigid external constraints. There is no purely 'natural' (i.e., irremediable) tragic contradiction between our nature and our circumstances. it would be rather odd if there were, because our tradition always said that there cannot be a purely objective and material contradiction, *contradictio in re*. Contradiction is a relation between propositions, and is therefore cultural. And so I am suggesting that although human life is indeed often riven with tragic contradictions, tragedy is cultural. It is bitter, difficult conflict within and among our values and our theories. But we can work at overcoming it, for example by redescribing bits of the world, by changing ourselves, or by revaluing things.

Many people will continue to protest that there are some basic facts of life, some ineluctable certainties. The two proverbially cited are death and taxes. Nobody will dispute that taxes are cultural. What of death? Cross-cultural studies show that it is very variously described and evaluated. To the poet Philip Larkin death was a terrifying nightmarish prospect all his life, but to someone else death may be a joyful deliverance into a better world, while to a third person death is promotion to the highest social status, that of a venerated ancestor. There are many different possible social constructions of death. Larkin's problem was not that he was going to die, but that he took a naturalistic view of death. It was unalterably dreadful, and he could see no way of escape.[1] But I am saying that there is a way of escape. Larkin's view of death is a cultural product, with a very familiar cultural history. It is too late now to do anything for poor Larkin, but for the sake of others who may still feel as he did, we need to make an early start to redesigning death. A wide-ranging historical and cross-cultural study will be a useful preparatory task, for it will give some notion of the range of what has been done. But it will not give us the answer that we need.[2] After it is complete, we must still accept full responsibility for our own cultural constructions, beliefs and values. Active non-realism says that there is no Nature, and the truth is not already laid on. Things are what you make of them and make them. The work of the aesthetic-religious imagination in the future will be to re-metaphorize the world. Our present woes are caused by certain intractable conflicts, clumsy constructions and negative valuations that we have inherited. To say that there is no nature is to say simply that these things are not irremediable. They can, with an effort, be changed.

(ii) What are we afraid of?

If as I have said every vision of the human condition is a local cultural construct, then we cannot go on pretending to produce universal philosophical descriptions of the human condition as such. Paul Tillich produced one of the last.[3] If he had said that his work was a poetic expression of Lutheran psychology, that would have been fine; but he claimed it was more. Today, we should know better.

What then is the alternative? I am advising an openly culturalist and therapeutic approach. We should not try to spin universal truths about the human condition as such out of our own entrails, by pure philosophical thought. There aren't really any such truths, and there isn't really any such pure and universal thinking either. Our strongest fears and anxieties are empirical rather than metaphysical, because the local culture always provides the forms in which they are felt. Furthermore, philosophies are also local cultural products. There is no universal and fully transcultural philosophical idiom. So we cannot make the distinction between a universal and metaphysical human condition on the one hand, and various local cultural supplements on the other. On the contrary, the metaphysical and the cultural and always bound up together, and cannot be disentangled. We cannot philosophize in any medium but language – which is always local.

So there's no reason to be ashamed of being empirical. You want to know what is wrong with us humans, and what we are afraid of? – then take a look at what in various cultures is accounted unclean and an abomination, and what arouses the greatest horror, disgust and dread.[4] The empirical evidence of ethnography suggests that people dread most the anomalous, the formless and the unnamable. Our cultural life is always a struggle collectively to impose a pattern upon experience so as to make a common life-world for us to inhabit together. We very much want everything to be classifiable and to have a clear identity that it keeps. We want the world to be orderly. There needs to be a general cosmic framework within which everything happens, grids on which everything can be plotted, binary distinctions which tidily polarize everything between complementary opposites, classification systems within which everything can find a slot for itself, laws that everything obeys, and values that always stand firm.

The means by which we try to set all this up is just language, a complex shifting system of finely modulated and co-ordinated behaviours and games.[5] Contrary to what is often thought, we haven't got a ready-made world laid on for us. Nor have we got values laid on. We have to build, and we have to do it by battling with each other and adapting our micro-behaviours to each other until we have settled habits, conventions, customs and patterns of order.

It is a continuing struggle. The world is always imperfect, uncomplete. But we dream of a successful accomplishment of the world-building task. Paradise, childhood, the Golden Age, heaven, utopia – these are visions of a stable well-ordered world in which there is a place for everything and everything is in its place. A harmonious world in which there is general agreement about procedures and values, and life therefore makes sense for everyone. Such a world, with its stable identities and values, would be a world on the gold standard; but our endless effort to establish it is haunted all the time by the fear of failure.

Do we see the problem here? It is that the very temporality of our life and our language, which makes our world-building possible, also makes it impossible finally to complete it. Time, which makes words possible, also makes a last word impossible. Perhaps this is life's most basic ambiguity. It gives rise to our perennial fear that our classification systems and our interpretative frameworks may not be adequate to order the chaos of experience. We are therefore afraid of failure and death; we fear, that is, that we may at the last be overwhelmed by disorder, corruption and the uncanny.

We can distinguish at least four different strands in these fears.[6]

(a) *Nausea.* Our attempt to order the world may fail if the world-stuff turns out to be too nauseatingly and obscenely formless, slimy, rotting, decaying, viscous, squelchy and disgusting for us to be able to get hold of it. In this case the world-stuff is too infuriatingly weak. It does not offer enough resistance to be a workable material. It is just repulsively shapeless and sloppy.

(*b*) *Horror* is the opposite case. When I am suddenly horror-struck or paralysed with fright, I am the one who finds himself weak and strengthless. I simply cannot move. I am like a man whose weapon has broken in his hands. My words and my interpretative frameworks are overwhelmed by a Power that seems to burst them apart.

So I am filled with nauseous disgust by slime that is too weak and non-resistant for me to be able to find words for it; and I am filled with horror by something that is too uncanny or *unheimlich* for me to be able to capture it in words. In both cases one feels a kind of impotence: in the first because the stuff out there is too weak for words, and in the second because our words are too weak for it. In complete contrast, there is now a third case in which the problem is that we are suddenly filled with an urge to take prompt and very violent action. This is the case where we feel:

(*c*) *Outrage*, anger and shock at a violation. The metaphors used imply that there has been a rape, a disgraceful and illegal intrusion. A prohibition has been broken, a barrier has been breached, a frontier crossed, a sanctuary violated and a mark overstepped. This sinful act creates a very serious situation of pollution or defilement. We are filled with an urgent impulse to act at once. It is necessary to wipe out, erase, and blot out the transgression – which means, in effect, the transgressor. And it must be done right away.

In this important case we see how the social world is structured by prohibitions, taboos and commandments. Some of these lines or rules are so important to use that the whole fabric of our world is threatened if they are violated with impunity. Rapid and perhaps extremely violent action must be taken to reassert the authority of the rules. Outrage, indignation and anger are as it were strong horror, for here we again feel a close and manifest threat to our whole construction of the world, but this time it is coupled with an urgent impulse to corrective action. We know just what we have got to do.

(*d*) *Awe* in the presence of what is sublime or mysterious is different again. Although it is a kind of fear, it does not involve either a sense of one's own impotence or a sudden rush of blood. Awe is a pleasurable fear, associated especially with silence. Words are not needed. We don't have to bark orders in an effort to master the situation. Our mood is attentive but not active. What is before us is like the sublime in art: it makes enough sense by itself and doesn't require any additional linguistic effort on our part. We feel both exalted and attuned.

Four sorts of fear, then, that we may experience when we find language somehow inadequate to its usual task of positing and maintaining a reasonably stable world-order. What I am up against fills me with nausea and disgust when it is too weak for words; with horror when words are too weak for it; with outrage when the whole language-established order of things has been violated and we must act at once to reassert it; and with awe when words are unnecessary. In each of these situations I may speak of being in the presence of something for which words fail me, something that is ineffable, wordless, indescribable, inexpressible, unspeakable or nameless.

In each of these cases, however, by saying that something is beyond language and by describing it, I have brought it within language. Our brief phenomenological analyses of some states of being at a loss for words were themselves, inevitably, articulated in words. So I wasn't really at a loss, at all.

The best way to resolve this paradox is to grasp that when we talk about what is beyond description we are not talking about anything like a quasi-geographical zone beyond a hedge or a fence. All our language here is dominated by metaphors of field-boundaries and lines of demarcation drawn on two-dimensional surfaces. Those metaphors are thoroughly confusing. There is no fence marking the limits of what can be said, and therefore there is no 'territory' on the far side of any such fence. Language really is outsideless, and it evokes all that it forms. So when we talk about the indescribable we are not talking about a world of pure not-yet-verbalized experience, nor are we talking about some supposed transcendent world of pure Being that language cannot reach. (That is a silly idea, because I just reached it.) No, what we are talking about is a current of anxiety and fear that accompanies all our uses of language, and which makes itself apparent in our language. Especially in our metaphors, as our little studies have just shown.

So when we attempt the seeming absurdity of trying to express in language our fear that language may be inadequate we are not obliquely referring to something beyond language. Rather, we are expressing time-anxiety. Language is radically temporal. Language and time each presuppose the other. Language-use makes us aware at once that we are continuously creating and ordering reality *and* that we are all the time failing to complete the task. Even as we utter language, we are filled with profound horror at its arbitrariness, emptiness, imprecision, lack of 'presence' and continual slippage into oblivion. Even as language-use produces reality it also reminds us of inevitable loss, as the sign itself keeps losing presence, losing closure, and losing grip on reality.

Our dissatisfaction is odd and paradoxical. There's no way we can build a world together except in time and with language. But the very conditions that are necessary to our enterprise also fill us with dread. Inevitably, our anxiety about time and language betrays itself in the language we use, and so becomes self-feeding.

Every sort of philosophical and religious wisdom will tell us that life's a package in which creation and destruction, coming-to-be and passing-away, life and death, presence and absence, gain and loss are bound up together. In every word of every sentence. And you cannot split the package. Nevertheless, we keep dreaming of splitting the package; and that is what is wrong with us.

(iii) The loss of value

Values were only ever really stable and secure in those societies, mostly ancient, which saw time as being cyclical. Earthly events tracked the unchanging and perfect round of the heavens and the seasons. The cosmos was a *perpetuum mobile*: every day, every month, every year, the wheels turned again and every thing on earth was rejuvenated.

In such a world-view the norms that guided human life were in the very highest degree natural and not cultural. Values just couldn't have been more cosmic, built-in and unchanging. They were also original and archetypal. People looked to the golden past rather than to the future. All standards had been set 'in the beginning', 'in those days', 'at that time'. Each year the annual cycle of festivals reunited everything with its own normative origin and thereby hallowed it. Nothing on earth was real or holy by virtue of being individual or new. Quite the opposite: every person and every sort of action was real and effective and sanctified only in so far as it participated ritually in its own archetypal ground.[7]

We tend to associate this cyclical-time cosmology with preliterate or at any rate pre-philosophical societies. Yet so powerful is the cluster of ideas involved that it remained influential throughout the Middle Ages, and almost up to modern times. Our culture has been queerly mixed: we have believed both in cyclical time and in linear historical time. Christianity in particular has conjoined elements of both outlooks. On the one hand it has been an eschatological religion which looks eagerly forward to redemption at the end of historical time; while on the other hand it has also been a 'traditional' faith with a strong doctrine of the heavens, a religious vision of the cosmic order, and a liturgical year that regularly renewed the participation of believers in the founding events of their faith. Only with the rise of our present science-based industrial civilization has the old cyclical-time cosmology faded away. By now our view of time is almost entirely linear-historical, and scarcely at all cyclical.

The legacy of all this, however, is that all historical societies have seen themselves as moving in a straight line away from Eden. The Age of Gold has been succeeded by Ages of Silver, Bronze, Iron and perhaps clay. Apart from the rather short period of Western belief in progress (1700-1968, at the outside), historical civilizations have seen history as a process of moral decline. Change means decay. People who think this way are still moral realists, for whom the old values remain objectively binding. The trouble is that as we move ever further away for Paradise, the ancient values recede steadily into the past, and each new generation has less and less respect for them.

What has happened here is that the old cyclical-time cosmology, occupying the moral high ground, has succeeded in casting a moral blight over history. Historical action departs from traditional norms. It is by definition innovative, and innovative action, being unprecedented, is unhallowed. To have departed from the sacred Origin is original sin. So the historical human being has always been conscious of sin, and has almost always believed that the world is in an advanced state of moral degeneration.

What, then, is new about our present-day experience of the loss of value? We need to make certain distinctions.

There is first the loss of valuable objects and persons. It is generally agreed that we should try to conserve valuable objects, species and landscapes, and it is widely felt that a powerful and loving God, if such exists, will surely conserve valuable persons. The general principle is that if you love something and can conserve it, you will do so. But it seems that precious things and people are disappearing from the world all the time, and this is a loss of value which is to be regretted.

Value-loss of a second type occurs when there is a steady decline in the strength of public commitment to certain values. The values as such remain unchanged, and perhaps are not openly challenged; but people's will to defend them is weaker than it was. However, we may find that in a crisis the old conviction and moral energy is re-activated, so this sort of value-loss may not be irreversible.

A third kind of value-loss happens through the decay of idealism and the spread of moral cynicism. Capitalism tends to reduce all values to prices, and in the advanced media society, public opinion, tastes and behaviour are constantly and very expertly manipulated for profit and political advantage. By helping market researchers, people cheerfully assist in their own manipulation. And indeed a rather jocular moral cynicism is very widespread nowadays.

However, none of these three sorts of moral loss – the loss of precious things and people from the world, the weakening of public commitment to certain values, and the spread of moral cynicism – none of these is especially novel. The first has in the past been met by keeping various records and erecting monuments, and by the religious belief in the *restauratio omnia*, the universal restoration at the end of time. As for the second and third types of value-loss, well, society could and often did recover from them.

Over the last century or so, however, a fourth and altogether more serious type of value-loss has come to be recognized. In the past we tried to picture our values as being solid and unchanging. They are not. They are very-finely nuanced, volatile, shifting, perspectival and situational. Historical change mysteriously alters the flavour or complexion of values. My values, which seem clear and straightforward to me today, may suddenly be destabilized by factors quite out of my control. I can have the value of my own values taken away from me willy-nilly. It has happened repeatedly in recent decades, and all the indications are that it will continue to happen. Just as we can no longer be sure that any set of beliefs about what is so will last a lifetime, so we can no longer be sure that the values we now live by will last, either. We have to live without any backing. We have to improvise, cobbling a faith together as best we can, and modifying it constantly.

It seems that most people find this unendurable, and prefer instead to join in some sort of collective flight to certainty. They embrace fundamentalism, nationalism, traditionalism, authoritarianism. Anything, so long as it seems to provide some sort of stable framework and set of values, through allegiance to which the self can achieve for itself a moderately stable self-definition.

But the flight to certainty is not a cure: it is a symptom of what's wrong with us. We don't like contingency, we can't bear the contingency of value, and we certainly don't want the responsibility of having continually to argue, reimagine and modify our own values.

The position is that in the late-modern world values have become like political convictions. We have to be flexible, pragmatic and ready to innovate. Nothing's fixed. But can we bear it?

(iv) Loss by choosing

A being that lives only in its own immediate experience, right up against raw sensation, cannot be aware of time. Its whole life is simply a this-now. Because it does not in any way transcend or stand back from the here-and-now, it has no view of anything other than this. It may well be capable of reflex responses to various stimuli and it may be equipped with useful inbuilt behaviour patterns, but it cannot be an agent that frames and executes purposes until it lives in time, and it will not live in time until it has been trained to function through general signs.

Cultural training, I am saying, works by hanging a veil of signs between us and pure immediacy. It introduces a little distancing which makes us capable of reflection, deliberation and intentional action. When we are no longer wholly absorbed in the sensations of the moment, we become able to contemplate possibilities and make choices. But we are aware of having paid a price. We have had to renounce the pure, intense timeless immediacy of prelinguistic experience, and there seems to be no way back to it. Indeed it has effectively ceased to exist, at least as far as we are concerned.

So how does cultural training succeed in separating us from pure immediacy? The answer is hard to state without invoking too many old and awkward technical terms, but it has to do with the generality of the sign. When we were first socialized and taken into the human cultural world (a process that we may picture as

94

happening in the first weeks of life) we were inducted into a world of signs with general meanings. A smile, for example. So thoroughly were we trained that today you and I cannot have an experience at all except in and through the activation of a general sign.

People think this doctrine of mine paradoxical.[8] But try to imagine an object presenting itself for which you really have no words at all. You can't affix any general label to any of its characteristics. You can't even say that it is an object with characteristics. Surely it is an un-thing? It does even manage to be a hallucination. It's utterly empty, null and void. It does not exist. For us who live in the world of signs, nothing is seen intuitively, worldlessly and purely as it is. The main Western tradition in philosophy always declared that only God sees things that way. His understanding is intuitive, whereas ours is discursive.[9] He sees things absolutely, whereas we see them only through general notions, that is, concepts. Or in modern terms, signs or just words. I don't see redness absolutely and purely individually. I see a red thing as 'red', that is, through the word 'red'. I can see only by classifying. My consciousness and my vision of the world are therefore always a bit gauche, generalizing, stereotyping and clumsy.[10] My vision is 'theory-laden', interpretative, perspectival. Raw immediate experience of the particular here-and-now has had to be lost so that our apprehension of the world can gain generality and form. We lose immediacy, we gain reflection. The sign has always in some measure had to be abstracted or distanced from its own particular material origins and circumstances, and therefore has become able to have effects beyond itself. Just by being general, the sign reaches out to other states of affairs elsewhere, perhaps in the past or the future. The sign is our only metaphysics, our little bit of transcendence.

All this is true, incidentally, not just for ordinary general words but also for proper names. The name Don Cupitt evokes not just the person who this second sits here penning these words but a lot of other past and future Don Cupitts too. Indeed, the name cannot be used successfully even this once now, unless in principle

it can also be used successfully on many other occasions. Single
fleeting instants are never given proper names. They can't be. The
attempt to name an instant, only once, would fail. So even proper
names bring time with them. And in general, any use of a sign
always implies the possibility of other previous and subsequent
uses of it.

Consider too how in the sentence the force of any particular
word is determined in part by what has already gone before it,
and in part by what follows. Meaning is contextual, which means
processual. Meaning is not delivered all at once, but over time.
So, again, the use of words in forming sentences introduces us to
temporality.

When we were children, even before we could speak our
induction into a cultural world of general signs had already begun,
and the movement of signs brought with it the passage of time.
Temporal continuity is a cultural artefact, produced by the way
the movement of signs runs. We see this particularly clearly if we
study the editing of cinema film and videotape. Continuity is a
cleverly contrived carrythrough from cut to cut that keeps the
narrative movement not only plausible, but also even-paced and
smooth-running in emotion, style and mood. And as in cinema,
so too in prose fiction temporal continuity is a product of
art. During the twentieth century cinema began by borrowing
techniques for producing temporal flow from oral narrative,
the stage and prose fiction. By the nineteen-thirties cinematic
techniques had advanced so rapidly and had become so powerful
that novelists like Aldous Huxley and Graham Greene began to
borrow them. Today audiences have become adept at handling
the running of three or more different time-scales simultaneously.
The case where there is a flash-back within the time of the action,
within the running time of a film, is relatively primitive: it would
be easy to find far more highly-elaborated examples. But this
extreme multiplication of timescales and techniques makes clear
to us the extent to which time is a cultural artefact.

For another angle on all this, consider such archaic narratives
as the myths of the Australian aborigines, dreams and *Gilgamesh*.

In these cases the narrative seems to us oddly jerky. Either the literary techniques for making time run smoothly have not yet been invented, or for some reason they are not being used. Either way, we are being made aware by contrast of just how highly-developed in our culture the various editing techniques have become. We are very clever indeed at making time, prose, film and life flow smoothly.

This in turn means that, like 'woman' in some of the writings of Kierkegaard, we are acutely aware of time slipping away and have a high degree of time-dread.[11] Living in a world of signs and living therefore in time, we know that on each occasion where we make one of our basic life-choices, the not-chosen at once becomes an eternally lost chance or possibility. Paradoxically, as we exercise our freedom to choose, we progressively narrow the scope of our own future choices. Time goes by and the options close. Once we had the world all before us: now there is less and less for us to look forward to. More and more we think about what might have been. Strange, that in the perspective of several decades we learn that the only freedom we have is the freedom to become this or that fixed and settled person who no longer has very much freedom, but is merely on rails to the grave.

So I am suggesting that our culture has become highly conscious of the passage of time and of loss by choosing. We are surrounded by lost possibilities and might-have-beens. We dream of childhood, of a tradition-based society and of a world in which there is no loss because time stands still. And we remain nostalgic for pure and prelinguistic sensuous immediacy, picturing it as a lost Eden from which we have been exiled. We seek contact with it through painting and music. Above all, it influences our religious thought. God has always been thought of as knowing all things immediately and intuitively without the mediation of general signs, as living in a timeless present (*nunc stans*), and as being both our Origin and our Last End. This means that God has symbolized a blissful primal state of wordless, timeless immediacy that we may be able to regain through the practice of religion. Is that not why religion almost always sees Heaven, eternal life or 'release' as a state beyond words, beyond time, beyond the duality of subject and object – and *therefore* utterly blissful? The aim seems to be to recover a state of consciousness that we think we enjoyed when new-born, or even before birth, and which we associate with God.

However, if I am right there is no consciousness before the sign has separated us from pure immediacy. The yearning nostalgia for wordless, timeless bliss is false because it cannot be satisfied. It is an incoherent longing. There is no paradise of pure immediacy that we have lost and might regain. We humans emerge only within the world of signs, temporality, choice and finitude, and it is a world with no outside. So we don't need a religion that works to alienate us from the only reality there can be for us. We need a therapeutic religion that reconciles us to our actual lot. We've got to learn to say yes to the sign, yes to temporality, and yes to the choosing that confirms our finitude.

On its philosophical side a therapeutic religion will keep on patiently showing the emptiness, falsity and illusoriness of all our old yearnings and discontents. But we humans are intractable beasts. We may be fully aware that the old yearnings are vacuous and harmful, and yet remain quite unable to shake them off. So there'll have to be religious practices as well, by means of which we train ourselves to like our lot. They may include the enacting of a myth of a god who decided to become an ordinary mortal human being because it was preferable. And our future religious practices will include a demonstration that the value of this our human life depends entirely upon the eyes with which you look at it. Look at it in a mood of ennui and discontent, and it is worthless; look at it with the eyes of love and mercy and it *still* has the infinite value we thought was lost.

(v) The loss of the self

If my correspondents are in any way representative, there has been a remarkable change in recent years in the religious outlook of older people. For several decades the standard view among social psychologists was that youth and age are very different from each other. Here is a typical statement from the mid-seventies, based on empirical evidence gathered during the previous forty years:

> The heightened religion of age is very different from the heightened religion of adolescence. In adolescence there is great intellectual perplexity and doubt coupled with emotional turmoil: young people suddenly change their whole orientation one way or the other. In old age, when intellect and emotions are limited, there is no worry about the niceties of theology, nor is there any emotional excitement about religious matters.[12]

And the same authors go on to note that among the elderly the percentage of the age-group who are 'certain of an after-life' rises to 100% in the nineties.

Today that picture of a serene dotage looks like a stereotype, and not only condescending but also wildly inaccurate. We are now finding that older people fit more closely the traditional description of adolescents, except that they are much more sceptical and less easily satisfied. After decades of being usually too busy to think, they are finding themselves suddenly retired, fit and vigorous with maybe twenty years of life before them. They have the leisure to philosophize: at least, they are wanting to fill gaps in their own education, and they are trying to come to terms with the way the culture has changed, almost without their noticing it, during their own lifetimes. They are asking themselves what they have achieved, whether they are satisfied, what their life has meant to them, and in what spirit they face its close. And they are discovering to their own horror that they don't actually believe anything any more. This realization plunges them into all the 'intellectual perplexity and doubt coupled with emotional turmoil' that is traditionally associated with youth.

They are saying to themselves something like this: 'I'm a blank.

I don't believe anything. We always thought that there has to be some good news about the world that makes life worth living. But where is it; and without it, where am I? There's got to be something that it's all in aid of, and I've got to know what it is. The drama of the life of a human self matters, doesn't it? Doesn't it? Back in the forties and fifties when we all read Graham Greene and Sartre, we believed in the self and freewill and we believed that your inner life was of infinite importance. You were confronted by great issues of good and evil, loyalty and betrayal. Your choices in the face of these mighty moral dilemmas fixed your eternal destiny. Life really did matter: do you remember how we worried about whether Scobie was saved?

'Now what has happened? I must have been too busy to notice, but somewhere during the past thirty years all the old absolutes and certainties seem to have turned out not to be absolutes or certainties at all, because they have melted and gone. The self, in the old sense, is dead. It has vanished like smoke. I've begun to notice that nowadays people seem to have only outsides, with nothing but a bit of purely secular emotional energy and machinery inside them. The old moral grandeur of life has been completely replaced by tinkering, by behaviour modification, media manipulation, issues, problems, adjustment and 'lifestyle'. God, how I hate that word. But morality as we used to understand it is dead. Death is dead too; it no longer matters. It just doesn't signify. It's not a bang, only a whimper. In the new culture the only values are those of image, appearance, vitality, youth and spending-power. There's upmarket and downmarket, and what else? As you get older and less economically active you get steadily less interesting, till by the time you reach my age you are totally invisible. Old age was once important; now it is simply inconsequential. It just doesn't count.'

My correspondent, who is a distillation from many originals, goes on: 'We used to think of people as two-levelled. Outwardly they might look pretty discouraging, pushed around by greed, lust, fashion, class mores, bad influences and political ranters. But somewhere underneath all that there always remained a possibility of freedom and a soul in need of redemption. However bad the appearances might be, it was a duty to believe that there was a deeper level at which something redeemable could be found in everyone. We used to say you should hate the sin but love the sinner. Today that distinction is dead. The sinner is the sins. People are only their own lives, their deeds, their external relations. The way they speak and the way they look is all there is to them. Look at the work of dramatists like Alan Ayckbourn, Caryl Churchill and Mike Leigh. Clever writers, but their characters don't have any insides. Life's become just a passing show. There is an exclamation of incredulous exasperation that people use: "Is that it?", meaning roughly, the mountains laboured and brought forth an absurd little mouse. After all the effort and the build-up, is that all there is? I feel like that. We seem to have lost morality and religion. Life has no depth: it's become just a media carnival that seems to be telling us that we too are just transient appearances who'll soon disappear. I find that impossible to accept. I'm going to follow up my hunch that there's got to be more to it all than that?'

So begins a furious quest. In the fifties the number of options that seemed to deserve serious consideration was small. Often it was a matter of just two or three. Today the range is so great that the search for an answer to life's riddle may seem like a borgesian quest through an infinite labyrinth. The problem is that a person who looks for a needle in a haystack knows what to look for and how to recognize it when it's found. She can specify just what the task is, how to perform it, and how to tell when it has been accomplished successfully. But in the case of the meaning of life we cannot state in advance what we are looking for, where to look, what method of search is appropriate, or how we will know that we have found what we are looking for.

My correspondents are therefore in acute difficulty. They are very restless. They feel an urgent desire to undertake a quest or pilgrimage, but they cannot spell out anything of the what, where and how. They can make no progress whatever, because they have no way of telling what might count as being even one step forward. Many are dying in despair. They are suffering from a generational distress like that of the 1860s to 1880s, the decades after Darwin's *Origin of Species*. For historical reasons our people still experience their distress as a metaphysical hunger that needs a metaphysical answer. But as we find they can't in fact spell out what they want or how they might be able to get it, we ought to consider another possibility. Perhaps their distress is a cultural condition which has a history, and needs a cure rather than an answer?

I have been suggesting that philosophical and religious thinking need to become culturalist and therapeutic in style. So let's go back a little, and ask how the present syndrome developed. Take down from the shelves the two volumes of Reinhold Niebuhr's *The Nature and Destiny of Man* (1941, 1943), or the three of Paul Tillich's *Systematic Theology* (UK editions, 1953, 1957, 1964). Alternatively, try the two volumes of Rudolf Bultmann's *Glauben und Verstehen*, essays from the thirties and forties later translated under the titles *Faith and Understanding* and *Essays Philosophical and Theological* (1969 and 1955). These are the last works of tolerable quality in which a version of the old-western Paul-Augustine-Luther doctrine of the self is presented in a way that might attract interest outside the narrow world of church theology. All three writers were of some general cultural significance. But their texts speak to us from a lost world.

An image of the way we have changed since the forties: in World War II people died under torture rather than betray their allegiances. Then the Korean War suddenly showed how easy it is to brainwash people. It appeared that there is no impregnable inner citadel of personal integrity. People cannot be expected to hold out. Nowadays, captured servicemen are very quickly induced to appear on enemy television denouncing their own countries. Everyone at home is most sympathetic, and at the end of hostilities the freed servicemen are received back home again without public reproach. They may even be welcomed as heroes. We now accept, it seems, that people are malleable, easily brainwashed in one direction and then debriefed back to normality;

programmed, deprogrammed and then rehabilitated. People are just the creatures of their own cultural milieux. Inwardness, consciousness, autonomy, moral allegiance, faith – all these things are no longer metaphysical. They are simply transient cultural inscriptions upon us. If we are suddenly transposed into a different cultural setting and find ourselves subjected to a different and quite clearly irresistible truth-power, we cave in at once. Our former inscriptions are effaced, and something else is inscribed upon us in their place. The conversion of a Western pilot in a Korean or Iraqi jail is just an effect of pressure.

We used to see ourselves as standing before eternal moral and religious realities, and we made irrevocable vows both in religion and in marriage. But today the self is an animal with cultural inscriptions written over its skin. And this skin-surface is a public space, a sort of screen or noticeboard on which others may read what we are currently giving ourselves out to be. The surface is communication, signs in motion. Below it, there is only a trembling of biological energies and responses. And that is what we are.

This new view of the self emerges in a line of thinkers who include Schopenhauer, Darwin (in his later works), Freud and Lacan. It is a sort of biological naturalism, it is a sort of semiotic materialism, it is a sort of 'post-Buddhism of the sign'. The self no longer stands out from the world, and indeed even the public-private distinction largely vanishes. The self is now just an effect of culture. It is a flux of images on a screen. It is its own communicative expression in the vocabulary provided by contemporary culture. We dance to the music of our own times: and that, dearly beloved brethren, is the simple truth – for today at least.

The new view of the self has triumphed in part because a whole line of thinkers have been busily chipping away at the old 'I-philosophy' of subjectivity or metaphysical individualism. This is a style of philosophy that everyone associates with Descartes, and indeed he did set out its doctrines with outstanding brevity and clarity. But he was not wholly original. After all, the whole Western tradition has seen the philosopher as an independent individual who stands a little apart from society and history and trusts only Reason. The ultimate touchstone and foundation is the rational individual's intuition of self-evident and necessary truth. So it had almost always been held, and Descartes was merely making the tradition more explicit and self-conscious when he claimed that the whole of metaphysics could be refounded upon the individual human mind's intuitive certainties about itself and about what is self-evident to it.

There is no doubt that Descartes' ideas still remain influential, especially in bourgeois Western countries – and especially in religious thought, where people are so inclined to believe that their own intuitions are giving them real information. But his sort of self – asocial, ahistorical, a thinking spirit which builds up a whole system of truth all by itself – is an impossible fiction. As a number of thinkers have argued, and very forcefully.

Consider first two papers published by the American founder of pragmatism, C.S. Pierce, in 1868: 'Concerning Certain Faculties Claimed for Man', and 'Some Consequences of Four Incapacities'.[13] Pierce puts forward simple and telling arguments to show that we are not justified in claiming to have direct, intuitive and certain knowledge either of our own existence as thinking subjects or of our mental states and operations, or of our own sense-experiences. On reflection it is clear that selfhood is always learned along with the use of the pronouns, that knowledge of our own mental states is inferential and dependent on the public language, and that sense-experience is not pure intuition because it needs a sign that interprets it in order to be enjoyed at all. So Pierce radically undermined the whole tradition that tries to base knowledge on founding principles which are guaranteed in their turn by their self-evidence to the self-founding human mind. It is a mistake to try to establish primitive fixed points beyond time and criticism. Instead, Pierce opens the way for a new tradition which says that knowledge is always networky, probabilistic, disputable and common. Knowledge is democratic: it is an evolving consensus among those who care about the topic in question. It's the state of the argument. And in this new account of knowledge private selfhood no longer plays any essential part as touchstone or foundation.

Secondly, we must briefly mention again the remarkable Nietzschean doctrine of consciousness. Cartesian consciousness is perfectly centred: it is self-founding, self-possessed and exactly coincides with itself. Nietzsche de-centres it, showing very clearly that consciousness is secondary, imperfect, dispensable, and comes along only after the real work has already been done. Pierce had similarly argued that consciousness is not foundational but was evoked in us by the speech of others: 'testimony gives the first dawning of self-consciousness',[14] he says. Nietzsche goes further: if consciousness is a cultural product, then we need to ask what it is for, and whether in fact it is a good thing.[15] For example, when we use it to imagine other people's intentions and their point of view, then it is probably doing a useful job because it enhances sympathy and co-operation. But when it is used by moral and religious institutions to make and keep us guilty and self-accusing, it is a menace.

The most vivid example of the creation of consciousness in others as a tool of power over them lies in the way that men have made women more highly self-aware, intropunitive and self-accusing, precisely in order to keep them weak and dependent. Men chose power for themselves, and thereby gave consciousness to women. Men chose dominance, and thereby gave women relatively more deviousness. In all matters to do with persons and personal relationships women tend to be smarter then men. But this doesn't necessarily give them more power; on the contrary the superior skill and cunning of women is the cleverness that is produced by, and is needed to compensate for, the lack of power. And this is an important observation, because the whole Enlightenment tradition tended naively to equate the increase of critical self-awareness with the increase of personal power and freedom. Not a bit of it. And now we see why in our Western religious tradition (Paul, Augustine, Luther, Kierkegaard) vivid self-consciousness has so often been associated with an awareness of being 'feminine', powerless and blameworthy, before God.

Maybe if we had less self-consciousness we might actually have more power and creative energy. In short, we have a hint here that the recent collapse of the old-western philosophical and religious conception of the self may be a blessing, and not a misfortune.

Thirdly, there are the criticisms of mind-body dualism put forward by Wittgenstein and Ryle.[16] I'm going to make the point here very briefly. Careful reading of Shakespeare's play *Hamlet* provides quite sufficient evidence to set in motion all the usual talk about Hamlet's psychology, his states of mind, what he's thinking, his intentions and so on. We may get into arguments about what's going on in Hamlet's mind at some point or other, and there is no way to settle such arguments except by appealing to the text. So, in this particular case at least, everyone will surely agree that 'the mind' is not a thing but an interpretation of text (and interpretations are always open to dispute and reassessment). Next, we need to see that the most famous of all readers of the human heart, Freud, sitting at the head of his couch listening to a patient, was in logically the same position. Like a literary critic, Freud was reading signs. Furthermore, the patient can only produce signs and Freud can only read them because they both inhabit a logically-prior common world of signs. The final step is the realization that I am in the same position in relation to myself. In trying to understand my own often rather peculiar behaviour and feelings, I have no privileged access.[17] I am trying to interpret signs, I am dependent upon an already-established public world of signs, and my reading of myself is always culturally-conditioned, partial and disputable.

Fourthly, I want to refer briefly to the young Derrida's criticisms of Edmund Husserl, put forward in the 1960s.[18] They are important because of the way Derrida has undermined the belief that there is a deep, and even an ontological, difference between someone who goes through the motions and someone who really means it. The distinction between letter and spirit, the lips and the heart, outward form and inner intention, has always been important in our religious tradition, and has also been widespread in the philosophical tradition. To this day we speak as if to make your reception of a sacrament, or your act of faith, or your moral action truly meritorious and effective you must put a bit of your inner self into it. You must act in a spirit of singlemindedness or wholeheartedness. You have to inject a shot of sincere personal commitment, will or intention into your performance in order to make it meaningful and give it life.

Husserl, a Cartesian and a Lutheran in background, took up these ideas and generalized them. In the end the clear meaningfulness of any linguistic or mathematical expression has got to be traceable back to an inner meaning-constituting act of consciousness. We are reminded of Kant on morality. In the long run everything depends upon inner, formative resolutions of the will. What in the privacy of my own thinking I know for sure I mean to mean is the ultimate ground of the meaningfulness of all public communicative expression.

Derrida's counter-argument is at bottom very simple. The original distinction between someone who goes through the motions and someone who really means it collapses because there is no way of really-meaning except by going through motions. That is to say, repetition or conformity to some publicly-established and recognized rule is just as necessary to constitute sincerity as it is to betray insincerity. More so, in fact, in so far as sincerity is consistency. The spirit isn't at a different ontological level from the letter, but is only a particularly disciplined and finely crafted arrangement of letters. Really-meaning it is simply being truly and consistently observant, that's all. So all the metaphysical talk about the need for an inner act of will or intention to 'animate' our outward words and performances is only myth, a confusing picture. And again the self disappears into the flux of public signs on its own surface.

I have produced four examples from different national traditions, American, German, British and French. They all point in the same direction. They are saying that a particular account of the self is no longer tenable. Abridging Ryle, what we are rejecting goes like this:

The official doctrine hails chiefly from Descartes . . . Every human being has both a body and a mind. They are ordinarily harnessed together, but after the death of the body the mind may continue.

The mind is not in space and its workings are not subject to mechanical laws. Its career is private. A person therefore lives through two collateral histories, one consisting of what happens in and to his body, the other consisting of what happens in and to his mind. The first is public, the second is private; there is a physical world, and there is a mental world.[19]

And we might add that the mind is somehow in contact with, and even fitted to inhabit, a world beyond space and time. For as well as constructing an inner model of the external world, the mind is also thought capable of intuitive knowledge. It knows moral and religious objects (and perhaps also makes aesthetic judgments) by intuition, and it has intuitive knowledge *a priori* of certain necessary truths of mathematics, logic and metaphysics.

Such a view of the human self has dominated much of the history of Western thought. True, the Aristotelian doctrine was not so dualistic as Plato. Nevertheless, a sort of supernaturalism of thought, which saw thinking as a non-physical and extra-linguistic spiritual activity, was more-or-less standard from Plato to Hegel. It begins to be tellingly criticized in the nineteenth century by such figures as Feuerbach, Marx, Pierce and Nietzsche. As late as the early 1950s, Ryle's book could still seem *avant-garde* and provoked fierce controversy. But today it is just commonsense.

Thus the feeling of my correspondents with which we began this section, that the death of the self has somehow occurred during the past forty years, is correct. It doesn't matter very much whether you think that the philosophers pick up vibrations from the general movement of culture, or whether you think that out in the culture at large people get a whiff of what's going on in the world of thought. Either way, a drastic change has occurred, the so-called 'death of man'. A certain view of ourselves and of our life has come to an end. We are ceasing to think in terms of a physical world of material bodies out there which is modelled or represented in a mental world in here. (At this point I tap my skull.)

The mind-independent world of bodies is going, because the world around us is now completely covered over with, shaped by and produced by our own theories, interpretations, signs. The body-independent world of minds is going, because we see now that it was only a lot of metaphors and mythical effects of language. There's no pure sense-intuition and no pure rational intuition: it is all interpretation and all historically conditioned. We ourselves and all our knowledge are radically immanent within history.

Much of the popular realistic metaphysics goes when we give up the ideas of substance, matter, mind, pure sense-experience and rational intuition. We are left with a world that is no longer a single cosmos, more a flux of interpretations, theories, perspectives, meanings, signs.[20] A cultural and historical world. It is a world that is very thin, very flat, and made of patterns of meaning. It is a 'post-Buddhism of the sign', and we are immersed in it.

This world is entirely temporal, and so are we. A single still from a cinema film doesn't give you a person. Rather, you need to see a number of sequences. There is no static person, present and known all at once. A person is a role in a play or a story, and emerges only over time. I can know a person only by seeing her functioning in various roles over a sufficient period, and I can describe her only in narrative mode and in her historical context. A person is not a substance, and cannot exist outside her own place. She is the range of possible stories that can be told about her life.

Even today, two centuries after the rise of the novel and the philosophy of Hegel, we still find it amazingly difficult to grasp the time of our life. The linguistic distinction between nouns and verbs keeps prompting us to suppose that there is a real distinction between what a person is, her qualities and traits, and the course of her life, what she does and what happens to her. But I'm denying that distinction. I'm saying that we just are the time of our lives. We are for the time being. We are, as it were, traffic intersections in the flowing communicative life of humanity. That is how it is. Have you lost something, and if so, what?

(vi) What have we lost?

So what is wrong with us, and in particular why are we so concerned about time, loss and death? The answer has to do with our own recent cultural history. Over the past two centuries or so everything has become historical, with the result that we Westerners have had thrust upon us an almost Buddhist sense of universal impermanence. Our tradition has not merely left us ill-prepared to cope with this, but in some ways has made it worse for us than for the Buddhists. The reason is that from the past we have inherited a very strong sense of linear time, ticking away with mathematical relentlessness in a straight line. Only, it is not now ticking away towards any final explosion or Goal of the cosmic process; it is merely ticking away, endlessly and meaninglessly, into universal dissolution and oblivion. Now that time has come to include everything, it is duly carrying everything away with it, including all truths, values and persons. Current scientific theory assures us that even protons are mortal. Nothing is conserved.

We had expected a great deal more than this. At the head of our tradition, Plato admittedly took a near-Buddhist view of the visible world. It was radically impermanent, a mere flux of phenomena. But beyond it he posited an eternal intelligible order of Reason, with all the qualities the heart desires. Evidently we detest weak boundaries, ambiguity, time and decay, because the world of Forms was just the opposite. Its denizens were very clear-cut, general, lucid and unchangeable. And this eternal world provided not only a cosmic ground of meaning, truth and value, but also an origin and a final home for the human soul.

The major subsequent influences upon our tradition all went to strengthen the optimistic presumption that we have a good, thick well-furnished world. Aristotle, Descartes and the tradition of scientific realism have argued that the visible world turns out to be much more stable, law-abiding and generally intelligible than Plato thought. Secondly, Christian theology claimed to provide the key to the cosmic drama that God was directing. God superintended the movement of linear time from Creation to the Last Judgment, guiding all events towards the fulfilment of a moral purpose.

Our tradition, then, has strongly predisposed us to expect to find ourselves in a real intelligible cosmos whose workings make moral sense, which is going somewhere, and in which persons and values are conserved. That is what we thought we were entitled to, and now we've lost it all. We expected objectivity, cosmic support, the rounding-off and perfecting of things and the perpetual preservation of all that is true, good and beautiful – but instead it seems that time destroys everything.

As we have been suggesting, our difficulties centre around our conception of time. During the arguments so far we have introduced the following five different notions of time:

Primal and sacred time is the time of archaic ceremonial societies, pre-literate and therefore pre-historical. In such societies people are absorbed in the cyclical movement of the generations and the seasons. One might say that there is no death or loss in such societies, because people's attention is wholly fixed upon sacred archetypes which year by year and generation by generation keep on forever renewing themselves. Ritual makes human life turn with the cosmic Wheel, and takes the individual up into what is universal and undying.

Linear eschatological time is a form of historical time that seems to be associated with the rise of prophecy and narrative scriptures. God is the chief historical agent, but his action is at least partly hidden. Through prophecy and scripture, God tells us what we need to know about the ways he is guiding things, and promises us that in the End – perhaps not too far off, now – everything will be put right.

The *linear progressive time* of the Enlightenment also moved towards a blessed conclusion – the totalization of all truth and the liberation of humanity – but it was believed that all this would be brought about by the working of purely immanent laws of historical development or whatever.

What we now have instead might be called *time for nothing*, a world in which there is no conclusion but only movement. Nothing ever gets finally completed, rounded-off and made permanent; everything eventually dissolves, peters out and disappears. In our postmodern universe nothing ever gets to be stable and selfsamely present. Rather, temporal movement is needed to constitute a being or a meaning. It never reaches complete constitution, for the very movement of time in and through which it is being constituted is also all the time bearing it away. Such is our time for nothing.

We have also briefly mentioned a fifth conception of time which I might call *Dōgen's Now*.[21] To explain it, start with the God of Western thought. God knows what time is, and he knows what the time is; but he is not subject to time. God lives in a standing present or eternal Now, with all the past and all the future before him. Similarly, for Dōgen, it seems, the practitioner of Zen should live in a standing Now in which the whole world past and future 'presences' itself to him.

Dōgen is notoriously difficult, but one interpretation of him might be this: he is an extremely non-dualist, developing the standard Malayana doctrine that *samsara* and *nirvana* are identical. So he's saying, 'As you meditate, let the flux of things presence itself nakedly and unopposed in you. In that flowing impermanence you have all things, past and future. It is the Buddha Nature. It is Enlightenment. There is no tense, because nothing goes absolutely. There is only a Now that keeps renewing itself. This is It; there's nothing but this.'

Holding tense to be unreal, Dōgen reminds us a little of certain

Western philosophers, such as the Cambridge philosophers McTaggart and Mellor,[22] as well as certain Western mystics. However, I cannot quite propose his style of Sōtō Zen Buddhism (or *zazen*) as the solution to our present difficulties. The problem is that although the whole Mahayana tradition is in a certain sense admirably non-realist, and although it has also been admirably aware of the opacity of language, it still seems in the end to try to go beyond language. In quiet seated meditation we divest ourselves of all vocabulary and let Impermanence presence itself in us, and this is It . . . and it is being claimed in language that a certain fulness of Presence is attainable beyond language that is not attainable in language. And that I cannot accept. We are even more profoundly compromised by the flux than Dōgen – at least, as I have interpreted him – appears to allow. So profoundly compromised that there is no presence and no Now, but only a never-completed coming-to-be which is also a slipping-away.

The diagnosis, then, is that we have been precipitated very recently (so recently that most people don't yet know it's happened) into an extremely thin universe for which our tradition seems to have done little to prepare us. Next, the remedy.

7

THE CURE

(i) *Turning around*

Tragedy is cultural, we said. There isn't a natural human-condition-as-such. All representations of the human condition are cultural constructions. In principle, they can be changed. If some feature of the human condition as you experience it is causing you trouble, then you should ask historical questions about how this way of seeing things originated, and why it is now causing discomfort. An historical genealogy of our present discontents will supply the right context in which to spell out the diagnosis and seek a cure.

In the past, when thinkers described the human condition, they wrote as if they thought they were reporting natural (i.e., extra-cultural and universal) metaphysical facts. Here, they seemed to be saying, are the parameters of the-human-condition-as-such. One favourite device pictured our life as being suspended between various polar oppositions. Paul Tillich has three such contrasts.[1] He calls them individualization and participation, dynamics and form, and freedom and destiny. He also mentions a few others: subject and object, spontaneity and law. And he seems to consider that he is able to take up a standpoint outside all the major traditions. The oppositions are supposed to be natural and objective circumstances of life. Tillich does not observe that it is we, rather than the Universe, who like to operate in terms of binary oppositions; and he fails to note that the particular oppositions he cites are merely topics of one literary tradition.

Kierkegaard is rather smarter. He produces a lot of old chestnuts: finite and infinite, classical and romantic, and so on. But he knows that these oppositions have histories, and seems more aware than Tillich that he's not just doing straight metaphysics. He is standing within a literary tradition and commenting on its problems. Thus, Kierkegaard says that the classical world was contented with the finite. The Formed, as such, *was* finite. Christianity in its striving to pass beyond the formed and visible world had a Romantic character. Romanticism 'overflows all boundaries'.[2] Christianity therefore can't help but keep running into paradox. It has inherited the vocabulary of classical philosophy, but has always striven to say things that that vocabulary will not let it say. Christianity wants to say that God is infinite, perfect Being; that he can in some sense be known by us, loved by us and have dealings with us, and that he is united with us in Christ. None of this, however, can be spelled out clearly and non-paradoxically in the vocabulary that has to be used. In particular, the Western tradition has never been able to explain how a finite human subject could know an Infinite Being.

So – as it seems to me – Kierkegaard has rather more literary awareness than Tillich. He has a good knowledge of the historical genealogy of the terms and contrasts that are most prominent in his own thinking. Kierkegaard sees that we can no longer pretend that philosophy and theology are somehow extra-cultural. On the contrary, we are always within a tradition that prescribes both the problems and the vocabulary that we must, for good or ill, use to tackle them.

Yet even Kierkegaard – I must admit – doesn't take the next step. If the human condition as we now perceive it is merely the legacy of our own past cultural history, and if it has become very uncomfortable, why don't we redesign it? We know something now of how fabulously varied different faiths, philosophies of life, and visions of the world and the human condition have been. Why don't we create what we want? We also know that in different centuries and cultural settings the same text may be read in an endless variety of ways. So why shouldn't we re-interpret and redesign our philosophical and religious traditions to fit our new requirements?

Kierkegaard doesn't quite go all the way. There seems to be a little more constraining objectivity out-there for him than there is now for us. We will not ask him to specify what it is, because he cannot. He hasn't got any extra-historical or extra-cultural vocabulary available to say it in. But we will not press him further. We will return to our problems with time, loss, death and the extreme thinness of our post-modern world. I am saying that our problems too have histories. We need a diagnosis and we need a cure. Even time and death are cultural constructions whose significance varies enormously in different societies and periods, and whether you take an optimistic or pessimistic view of the human condition depends heavily upon your prior expectations.

We have suggested that time is by no means always seen as the great destroyer. In archaic cyclical time all things are regularly rejuvenated. In linear eschalotogical time there may be a short-term appearance of decline, but it is promised that when the End or Parousia comes there will be a universal Restoration and everything will be put right for ever. In linear progressive time there is an immanent working-together-for-good of all things. In the past there have doubtless been in our cultural tradition some elements of all three of these ideas. But during the present century we seem to have lost them all. We are totally cut off from the archaic universe, and we no longer experience our own linear sort of time either as moving towards a supernatural Consummation or as automatically delivering the universal liberation of humanity. We cannot seriously suppose that the sum total of human wretchedness is going to lessen much. The odds are, alas, that it will increase greatly. We are left with the prospect of endless unrequited human suffering, and with linear time ticking on into universal dissolution and night. Furthermore, we have during the past two hundred years come to see all faiths, philosophies, truths and values in historical terms. Everything now is a product of time and chance – and everything therefore gets carried away by them.

Yet this prospect does not have to make people pessimistic. There have been plenty of Western and Indian sceptics, phenomenalists, acosmists and so forth who have managed to be light, good-humoured and even saintly within equally thin or even thinner visions of the world. But our problem is that our whole tradition has led us to expect a lot more. If the changing, sensuous world below looked dark and unstable, well, you took refuge in an unchanging ideal world above where truth and values stood firm. In our tradition we have believed in belief: we have thought that to make life bearable we need a set of tenets or dogmata assuring us that there is a deeper level at which things are better than they appear on the surface to be. We have believed that realistic beliefs are needed to make life worth living, and we have regarded a state of belieflessness as pitiable.

But now we are in it. We experience the radical impermanence and belieflessness out of which a Mahayana Buddhist makes beatitude; but it is not blessed for us. We experience it with an acute sense of crisis and loss, because our whole history has left us with all the wrong expectations and the wrong training.

Because we still have all those old expectations, the old beliefs that we have lost can still seem to be intelligible and very attractive. We may turn hopefully to religious authority, to fundamentalism, or to conservative nationalism in the hope of getting the old reassurances back again. It doesn't work, because the old beliefs are now too out-of-keeping with the way the world is. Much better to seek a cure for our old and now badly-misguided expectations. But we will only finally free ourselves from the old outlook when we have a new one that works better. We want a new religion that makes liberation and bliss out of the way the world now is.

Here's the first formulation: for a beliefless world that is *rightly* beliefless, we'll need a beliefless religion. Some wish to reinstate the old order, and claim that on my own premises I've got to admit that it might be done. Yes: but only as a fiction that might forget itself and stick. I don't want that. My aim will be different: let us attempt so to redesign ourselves and our tradition that we can make bliss out of pure transience. That's more like it.

(ii) Therapies

Suppose then that we are indeed in some very general and pervasive way troubled about life. We may feel a haunting anxiety about life's uncertainty, about freedom, and about the irrevocability of each passing moment. We may be oppressed by the vast weight of human evil, suffering and futility. We may feel horror at the thought of death and universal decay and dissolution. Or perhaps what troubles us most may be the feeling of weightlessness we get when life seems to us to be a very, very thin flux of seemings, void and insubstantial. If we feel troubled in these ways – and no doubt most people are, at some time or other – then what is the remedy? Or rather, in what ways might such a condition be cured?

By and large, people in the West are able to recognize only one type of answer to this question. To cure your discontent and make you feel your life's worth living, you need some good news to offset the bad news so far. This good news is supplied by doctrinal or metaphysical beliefs based on the appearance-reality distinction. That is, the remedy takes the form of an assurance that deep down the situation is much, much better than it looks on the surface. All the features of our life that were troubling us are consigned to the level of surface appearances, seemings or phenomena. Religion tends to associate this superficial level with the senses, materialism, the flesh and what is perishing or corruptible. We were right to feel strong dissatisfaction with this apparent or manifest order of things, because it is not our soul's true home and lasting truth and value are not to be found in it. Happily, behind the unsatisfactory world of appearance there is an enduring invisible substrate, the Real World. That is what we should cling to; that is our true home. The news about it is all good. It is a world of eternal reality, objective Truth and Value. It is a world of light.

Conceptions of the way the Real World undergirds the world of appearance are very varied – but the general theme keeps on recurring. A thing's visible qualities may change, but beneath them there is a substance that remains unchanged. Particular events in the visible world are made intelligible when they are shown to be governed by a general and unchanging invisible principle, a law of nature. A friend's speech and visible appearance may be very changeable, but behind them we discern a relatively unchanging self, mind or character, a set of thoughts, habits and intentions. The manifest evils of life, and the ups and downs of fortune, are explained and justified by reference to God's hidden and unchanging Providence.

In these and dozens of other cases, the same therapeutic idea is being called upon. Yes, the visible or manifest world is indeed unsatisfactory, and there is only one cure. We need to move beyond the visible to a better, invisible realm that lies hidden behind it. This better world is a world of *theory*, perceived with the eye of the mind. And it is the Real World, which is why the whole way of thinking involved here is called 'realistic'. It involves belief in an invisible Real World of unchanging and objective Truth, meanings and values, which is hidden behind the veil of sense.

How are we able to have access to this better world? Philosophy has commonly held that unaided human reason is able to recognize the timeless standards of truth, intelligibility and value by which our life should be guided. In religion it has often been held that at some time in the past the supernatural world broke through into this world and made itself known. Either way, we human beings are amphibians, denizens of two worlds. The world of space and time, the world of everyday life is indeed transient and very imperfect, but we are able to make sense of it and to live good lives in it in so far as we keep in contact with a better world beyond, a Real World of unchanging Truth and Values.

I insist that even to the present day these ideas remain very potent – perhaps especially among scientists. People in the West are imbued with the notion that there can be only one form of compensation for the unsatisfactoriness of the everyday world. We need *belief*; we need mentally to lay hold of something formative, something unchanging and intelligible that underlies the flux of appearances. We cling to our realism, and we cannot quite believe that any other sort of remedy could work.

For around two millennia Western culture has been dominated by Plato in philosophy and by credal, supernatural belief in religion. That is why we still tend to think that (whether it is in fact available or not) one thing and one thing only can make sense of life, namely doctrinal or metaphysical belief, based on the appearance-reality distinction.

But is realistic belief in fact a therapy that works? Bluntly, can realism save? Equally bluntly, the answer is simply No.

First, our exposition of realism has, I hope, shown how closely it is tied in to a certain traditional picture of the human subject's place in the world. The self stands alone. Its first question is: 'What can I know?' Knowledge begins with sense-perception, but turns out to require something additional to what comes through the senses. As well as the visible, then, there must also be something superadded, which is invisible. Now we begin to contrast the visible realm that is seen by the carnal eye with an invisible realm beyond, seen by the mind's eye. A whole series of binary contrasts then start to be made: the apparent and the Real, hither and yonder, the surface and the depth, outer and inner, flesh and spirit, the changing and the unchanging, literal and metaphorical vision. Language seems constantly to be reminding us of these contrasts – and now we begin to grasp the extraordinary extent to which the entire structure is a linguistic fiction. That is to say, the realism that has dominated our culture for so long has consisted in the entrenchment within the uses of language of a whole set of idioms, contrasts and metaphors. We have been ruled by these ways of speaking and these images. And when this is recognized, language has been discovered. We begin to see that our whole being is shaped by the linguistic tradition within which we stand, and that language has 'its own thickness, density, body, its own rules and unruliness'.[3] This fatally undercuts the primitive old picture of the single self, seemingly without language and alone in the world, using nothing but its physical senses and its Heaven-guided reason to construct its knowledge. The old picture goes, and therefore the appearance-reality distinction goes – and therefore realism also goes. It goes, because it is redundant. Language doesn't have or need a Beyond in the same way that sense-experience has to have a Beyond. Language, so to say, already presupposes and produces a world all by itself.

I've got to explain this last point, because most people miss it. They think that just as individual sense-experiences need some sort of supplementation from Plato's Real-World-Beyond in order to make them into knowledge, so words also need a similar supplementation. But this is not so. Language is already communal, and already contains all we know. Linguisticality is a world in itself. It is complete. Language is not 'mere appearance', and there is no self-consistent way of saying in it that there is something radically wrong with it.

Now do you see what I'm saying? The old picture of the seemingly-languageless single self alone in the world, using its bare senses and its bare reason to build knowledge, and setting up therefore a sense-reason, appearance-reality philosophy – all *that*, which ruled us for millennia, was able to rule us only for so long as we didn't recognize that it was only a myth produced by an age still unaware of language. Once we become aware of language, the old outlook is displaced or decentred. We have to invent new idioms. The new awareness of language that we have been given by Nietzsche, Heidegger, Wittgenstein, Foucault, Derrida and others has ended realism, because it has ended the old sense-experience-plus-concept theory of knowledge. Today, knowledge is linguistic.

Realistic beliefs can therefore no longer work as a cure for our world-woe. Rather, realism is itself a disorder of which we need to be cured. Which brings us to the second argument, which is that realism was in any case never a very good medicine. For it leaves the manifest world in exactly the same blighted and derelict condition as before. The situation is perhaps even worse than that: strong supernatural faith so insistently defers all perfection and value to the World Beyond that it makes realistic believers into something like damned souls, who take a view of life that is it anything more blackly gloomy and pessimistic than that of unbelievers. Isn't all this painfully familiar from Luther and Calvin, Pascal and Kierkegaard, Mauriac and Bernanos, Greene and Waugh? The more ultra-orthodox the Christian, the *less* the world is redeemed. Realism doesn't save the world; it damns it. What the most orthodox have called true religion has often been hatred, a pathological hatred of life.

Thirdly, realism does not liberate the self, either. On the contrary, it produces what the Buddhists call 'clinging', the psychological state of being hooked, fixated or attached. In the most extreme cases, where the attachment to some invisible object has become most rigid and fanatical, we speak of fundamentalism and rightly diagnose a serious religious disorder. But in all cases realistic belief is religiously retrograde. The realistic believer is religiously worse off and further from salvation than is the free and open-minded sceptic.

The fourth and last argument is a very simple one. The language of realistic belief is always a ruling-class language of power and control. It is not the language that is used by the great religious teachers. They tell stories and use rhetorical devices in order to bring about change in the hearer. That is, their sayings are designed to change the angle from which we view ourselves or our world. They want to change our values, or to change the metaphors under which we see things. They see us as being caught up in some sort of illusion, attachment or false construction, from which they want to liberate us. In the Madhyamika (the Middle Way) the error from which we need to be saved is explicitly diagnosed as realism.

I conclude from all this that realistic belief has been tried and tested pretty thoroughly in the Western tradition, and has been found not to work. It leaves the world unsaved and the self hooked.

In retrospect, there was in any case something very odd about the moves involved. The starting point was a pessimistic reading of the human condition, and the world-woe to which this led. The remedy was to accept that pessimistic reading so far as it went, and then to claim that there is a hidden, deeper and more real level at which the news is good, so stunningly good as to outweigh all the surface bad news. As the hymn says:

> Ye fearful saints, fresh courage take;
> The clouds ye so much dread
> Are big with mercy, and shall break
> In blessings on your head.
>
> Judge not the Lord by feeble sense,
> But trust him for his grade;
> Behind a frowning Providence
> He hides a smiling face.

On this account the appearances remain admittedly black. World-woe is not actually cured at all: it is merely repressed by a determination to believe that things are not what they seem, a determination that hopes one day to be vindicated. Meanwhile empirical appearances – 'feeble sense' – are not to be trusted.

This is an appallingly divided religious outlook: no wonder poor Cowper went mad. Subjectively, he is forcing himself to believe against the evidence, invoking faith against sense. Object-ively, the appearances are grim: dreadful clouds and a frowning Providence. But Cowper hopes one day to see blessings and smiles. Alas, he has not got salvation through his religion; he is merely clinging to a promise of salvation, one day. Meanwhile his world-woe is as bad as ever, and he must keep it in check by believing against it – which only stores up more and worse psychological trouble for him in the future.

So realistic belief is not actually salvific or therapeutic at all.

Are there any other options? The Western tradition contains at least a number of significant hints.

The first is found among the Epicureans and sceptics of antiquity. Both of these groups sought tranquillity of mind, *ataraxia*, and both regarded realistic dogmatic belief as unhelpful. The Epicureans summed up their outlook in the 'fourfold remedy', as they called it: 'God unterrifying, death unworrying, the good accessible, the bad endurable.' The Epicurean way of life was low-profile, pursuing not passionate love but friendship, and not wealth and power but retirement and private life. The sceptics, going a step further, considered that doctrinal or metaphysical belief was positively harmful, and that belieflessness made for happiness. The evidence as to whether that is true or not is mixed. David Hume gave perhaps the most famous example of a serene sceptical death. On the other hand, the latest commentary on Lucretius finds that his text, 'a struggle against anxiety, and particularly anxiety towards death', is not wholly free from the fears it combats.[4]

There is well-known comic sketch in which a malicious aircrew reduce a planeload of passengers to hysteria by repeatedly assuring them that there is nothing to worry about. Perhaps Lucretius does press a little too hard his arguments to show that the human condition is tolerable and death is nothing to fear. But many philosophers have shared his view that in contemplating the majesty of Nature and the transience of human life we can find rest for our souls; and there is something to be said, surely for the sceptics' claim that the zealous, committed believer is often tense and unhappy. Some Western sceptics, indeed, have come close to the Mahayana doctrine that attachment to metaphysical beliefs, far from being the way to salvation, is actually the evil from which we need to be saved.

The view that we need to be cured of belief is not confined to sceptics. Immanual Kant, as is well known, first turned Plato's Real World of Ideas into an order of transcendental concepts, and then argued very forcefully that they cannot be validly employed beyond the bounds of sense. There is only one recipe for objective knowledge; it involves applying concepts to experiences in accordance with rules. This limits objective knowledge to the empirical world and the various sciences of it. As for the ideas of dogmatic metaphysics and religious belief, because they cannot be fully cashed in the world of experience they must be understood as guiding ideals which embody various moral and intellectual values. As such they have a useful part to play. But they do not tell us how things are in a hidden world beyond the world of experience.

Kant seeks to convince us that supernatural or metaphysical beliefs are illusory. They involved hypostatization or reification.[5] Frankly, they are fantasies. Kant wishes us to accept a purely immanent and ethical account of religious belief. Its meaning for us consists in the way it guides our moral life and directs our aspirations in this world. Similarly, Kant wishes us to be content with a purely immanent or transcendental metaphysics of experience. He is a genuine therapist who seeks to reconcile us to our human condition by showing the contradictions we are led into by our natural but misguided attempts to escape it.

Kant's therapeutic method is taken much further by Wittgenstein. Kant's elaborate apparatus of concepts that we must apply to experience is replaced in Wittgenstein simply by language – not only its vocabulary, but also its communal character, the games we play in it, its structure and so on. All words get their meanings simply from the roles they play in the life of the sociolinguistic communities in which they are used. Wittgenstein's outlook is therefore radically immanent. Words work properly only when functioning in their natural theatre of operations, the arena in which they evolved and at home. Kant limited metaphysics to transcendental analysis: Wittgenstein limits it to grammatical analysis. He is not sympathetic to world-woe, metaphysical systems or dreams of transcendence. These are conditions that need to be cured. Wittgenstein aims continually to return us into ordinary language, the life world and the centre of things. His philosophy is genuinely religious in so far as it is a soteriological practice that persuades us to give up world-woe.

He seeks continually to return us into ordinary language and the life-world, in such a way as to persuade us that it is the Centre and Ground of things that we were looking for. I mean only that in the transactions of everyday life, and nowhere else, are all the norms of meaning, value and sanity established and maintained. Wittgenstein rightly thought of this insight as Jewish. A practice-religion, a religion of righteousness. Every day, on millions of occasions, one human being bumps into another and there is some kind of communicative exchange. That is the building block out of which everything is built. The conventions slowly evolved through such interactions are the only norms we have. Generalized world-woe and discontent with the human condition is meaning-less because we don't know and can't know of any other way that things might be. Our condition is outsideless, and discontent is pathological. So the aim of philosophical and religious practice must be to cure factitious and self-indulgent discontent, and to return people again and again to the only Centre.

Wittgenstein believed his own philosophy to be highly original, a new subject. In Western terms it no doubt was rather novel; but not in Eastern.

> Sāriputra, both the goal and its full realization are simply everyday realities. From the perspective of the highest mean-ing, however, there is no goal and no full realization.[6]

In the first of these two sentences the goal of all religious practice and teaching is said to be to return us into the practice of everyday life and a purified love of this world. In the second sentence, teleological thinking is overcome, and the daily practice of religion becomes itself the only goal of religion.

In the tradition that descends from Nagarjuna, the therapy consists in a practice that leads to the realization of an identity. The diagnosis seems to go like this: we humans have constructed our world by setting up a lot of distinctions and binary oppo-sitions. We contrast the end and the means, the higher and the lower, the primary and the secondary and so on. Our language and our ways of thinking divide up, hierarchize and objectify not only our world, but also ourselves. We become alienated and unhappy. We need a deconstructive practice that works to undo all the opposition and alienation. It effaces the lines of division, integrates and reconciles. Now and again we get a glimpse of the aboriginal, ineffable unity of all the opposites. That is Enlightenment, *satori*.

If the aim of religious practice is to gain a soul-healing glimpse of the unity of all opposites, then we can see why Buddhist teaching takes the form it does. For example, Yūhō Yokoi presents his summary of Dōgen's teaching in the form of eleven affirmations of identity. The first is 'identity of self and others'. In the *Genjō Koan* section of Dōgen's major work, the *Shōbō-genzō*, this is explained as follows:

> To study the Way is to study the self. To study the self is to forget the self. To forget the self is to be enlightened by all things. To be enlightened by all things is to remove the barriers between oneself and others.[7]

The explanation is presented in the form of a series of four interlinked insights. Religious practice ought to make us so calm, selfless and attentive to others that all moral barriers between us and them drop away. We become altruistic.

The outline of Dōgen's thought as a whole goes:

1. Identity of self and others.
2. Identity of practice and enlightenment.
3. Identity of the precepts and Zen Buddhism.
4. Identity of life and death.
5. Identity of *Koan* and enlightenment.
6. Identity of time and being.
7. Identity of being and nonbeing.
8. Identity of Zen Buddhism and the State.
9. Identity of men and women.
10. Identity of monks and laypeople.

11. Identity of the *sutras* and Zen Buddhism.

Of these eleven, numbers 2, 3, 5 and 11 aim at undoing instrumental or means-end thinking. When you are engaged in some practice or other, don't think of it as a mere means to the end of enlightenment. Engage in it whole-heartedly, for practice *is* enlightenment, and after the moment of enlightenment, practice continues. Numbers 1, 8, 9 and 10 seek moral equality and identity in social relations. Numbers 4, 6 and 7 are the most metaphysical and subtle of the identities. They spring, no doubt, from the old maxim of Nāgārjuna:

Samsara is nothing essentially different from nirvana.
Nirvana is nothing essentially different from samsara.
The limits of nirvana are the limits of samsara.
Between the two, also, there is not the slightest difference whatsoever.[8]

The Western equivalent of all this is the doctrine that God is immanent in all things. This may lead us to ask: If God is already immanent within us, why should we strive to draw nearer to him? Are we not already as close to him as can be? Similarly, if God is almighty and already controls all things, so that nothing happens or can happen apart from his will, why do we bother to try to discover and do God's will? Aren't we doing it anyway? And similarly, if samsara, the world of death and rebirth, is already nirvana, why is the struggle for nirvana such hard work?

Dōgen himself testifies that he was first intellectually awakened at the age of fourteen by a version of the same question. If all human beings are naturally endowed with the Buddha-nature, why should we have to battle so hard to realize something that's true already? I am suggesting in reply that Dōgen's identities may be seen as therapies. Our propositional and objectifying ways of speaking carve up the world, quite literally alienating one thing from another all over the place. The aim of religious practice is simply to unify all that has been split and divided. The enlightenment that religion seeks is a momentary 'non-thinking' glimpse of an ineffable primary unity.

Let's explain this in words, if we can. In his doctrine of time-being/being-time, Dōgen wants us to see how radically temporal being is. There is only the impermanent, but there is always the impermanent. Whatever is, keeps on coming to be; and it's keeping on coming to be is also always and inseparably also a passing away. That's being-time. Being is, as we've already remarked earlier, *processual*. And we know nothing else but this always-deeply-interfused unity of being and nonbeing, life and death, being and time. Life is life and death is death, and we should not think of them as being *opposed* to each other. It's all one package, eternally temporal, forever just now. We tend to think of time as going past or flying away, and therefore have a feeling of loss. But this is a mistake. In spring, everything is springtime: time-being abides in each moment and nothing is really either arriving or going away.[9]

Thus Dōgen; but he's not, of course, suggesting that our world-woe can be cured just by a text. The text itself keeps demanding whole-hearted and resolute practice. So the therapy is: 'Are you unhappy and divided? Are you suffering from acute world-woe? Then commit yourself to continual practice formed by this text, and you'll find the cure in the practice.'

This brief sketch of Dōgen's soteriology suggests the possibility that Christianity might come to be interpreted along similar lines. We would give up the grand cosmological claims and the realistic dogma. Instead, we would concentrate on salvation, summarizing the way in a series of identity-statements like Dōgen's. A few obvious examples:

1. Identity of loving God and loving one's neighbour.
2. Identity of faith and works.
3. Identity of this life and Eternal Life.
4. Identity of the holy and the common.
5. Identity of perfect self-affirmation and perfect self-surrender.

6. Identity of time and eternity.
7. Identity of dying and living.
8. Identity of creativity and receptivity.

Here then is our first statement of the remedy for the unsatisfactoriness of the human condition. *Not* supplementary information about another realm of being, but a practice that strives to reconcile and unify our divided condition.

(iii) Impermanence

According to David Hume, we are 'nothing but a bundle or collection of different perceptions, which succeed each other with an inconceivable rapidity, and are in perpetual flux and movement. Our eyes cannot turn in their sockets without varying our perceptions. Our thought is still more variable than our sight; and all our other senses and faculties contribute to this change; nor is there any single power of the soul, which remains unalterably the same, perhaps for one moment. The mind is a kind of theatre, where several perceptions successively make their appearance; pass, re-pass, glide away, and mingle in an infinite variety of postures and situations. There is properly no *simplicity* in it at one time, nor *identity* in different . . . '[10] And Hume goes on to add that 'the comparison of the theatre must not mislead us.' We know how a play is staged in a theatre, but in the case of the mind we do not know how or where the goings-on are staged. On the contrary, the mind is constituted only by its own perceptions, and we have no notion of where they are occurring or what they are made of.

Today, we cannot quite accept Hume's wording. His talk of 'the mind' seems to suggest an inner-outer distinction which we have no sufficient reason to make. What he calls 'the mind', I call the point of view of experience, and the events that he sees as taking place in my mind I see as taking place out there before me, and in view. The mind is not a thing or an inner space but merely a point of view, an angle on the world. That quibble apart, Hume is right to stress that if we will but pause to consider we will be filled with wonder at how fast-changing, how miscellaneous and disorderly is the realm of immediately-given experience. We don't see this at first, because we are unaware of the continuous constructive activity of the brain, busily filing up all the gaps and interpreting fresh input in the light of the extremely complex world-hypotheses we carry around with us. This activity of the brain is so extensive as to conceal the true situation. For the stable and well-ordered world that we take ourselves to be dealing with is no longer the world of immediate experience. It has been thoroughly laundered. Immediate experience is far too disorderly to give us such a world. The world we have got is a fiction that we have posited, the world of our own world-hypotheses.

Put it this way: the new-born child's first experience is nothing but a blooming, buzzing confusion, without any structure. but within a few weeks the child is able to respond to the general pattern of a human face, and according to Piaget (whose view seems still to be generally accepted) at the age of six months the child appears to have formed the notion of 'object permanence'.[11] So far as immediate experience is concerned, mother (for example) is not presented to the child as an enduring self-same person. Experience gives only intermittent and very fast-changing apparitions, part-visual, part-auditory and part-tactile.[12] At some stage, however, the baby needs to form the hypothesis that mother is a single permanent object who continues to exist even while she's out of range. The age usually given for this notion is around six months, because it is at that age that the child will first look disturbed if two mothers – perhaps the genuine one and her identical twin – seem to appear by the cot. Thereafter, and with the help of the group among whom it grows up, the child progressively develops and elaborates its world-hypothesis. Language-acquisition is the key event, grammar, syntax and narrative prescribing a very complex world-picture. Soon the child has developed a complex theory of its own immediate physical and moral geography. It reaches the stage where it lives primarily, not by immediate experiences, but by its world-hypothesis. This world-hypothesis is decently stable. Predictions can be derived from it. It works; and increasingly it comes to be relied upon. Immediate experience now, for most of the time, is not doing any more than activate or switch on a small area of the hugely complicated map-and-lexicon that the child has at its disposal.

The child has now reached the normal adult condition. It thinks it lives in a fairly stable physical world of persons and things with various qualities, moving about in a framework of space and time. But this world, the world of our world-hypothesis, is in truth nothing more than a communal cultural and linguistic fiction. It is, perhaps, consistent with sense-experience – but the same could undoubtedly be said of countless other cultural systems. Certainly it is very useful; indeed, it is necessary for our social life and for our survival. It seems so real to us that we easily forget its fictioned status. We live in it and by it. The world of immediate experience is far too chaotic and disorderly to support our life. Indeed, we cannot really get back to it any more, because if we strip away all the language, all that *forms* our experience, then nothing is left but white noise. In fact, as we have said, immediate experience now functions as no more than a trigger or switch. The world or worlds we inhabit are highly-developed cultural creations.

We should add that the culturally-posited world that we inhabit need not be thought of as a lot of inner or 'mental' maps, models and reference books. It is sufficient to regard it as a lot of socially inculcated linguistic and behavioural capacities and dispositions. As such they serve us very well, most of the time, and we continue to revise and update them as needed.

There are, however, some snags. The principle of object permanence leads us to suppose that we've got a world that somehow manages to combine being temporal with being pretty stable. A world of beings *and* time, nouns *and* verbs, substances *and* events. We get caught up in a confused and paradoxical ontology. In the Western tradition, for example, a relatively-independent being is called a substance, and being is contrasted with (temporal) becoming, all in such a way as strongly to suggest that any real being should be timeless and unchanging. This in turn leads us into some very awkward linguistic habits. We want to represent the human person, or at least the soul, as a finite substance that remains self-identical through time. We believe in personal identity, and speak of the person as living 'in time', as if time were an extraneous element or milieu like water. So Cupitt, a basically timeless being, lives 'in time' pretty much as an otter, though basically a land animal, lives in water. Living in time, I admittedly become in some measure *subject to* change and corruptibility. I act, I take part in events, I am now in a state of sin, and now in a state of Grace. So I am bound to concede that I do change a bit. But all this is now getting us into some difficulty, for part of our language seems to be suggesting that we are self-identical substances and basically unchanging beings, while the rest of our language seems to be suggesting that we are radically temporal and therefore are nothing but our own life-stories. We are the lives we have lived and the roles we have played; we are our stories, with nothing whatever about us that is guaranteed to remain identical and unchanging.

The confusion has arisen because the felt need for object permanence has led us to postulate a very muddled world, part unchangeable and part changing. We think of the world as containing both nouns *and* verbs, both beings *and* time ('in' which they live), both substances *and* events.

We see now that culture has, and perhaps cannot help but have, a queer inbuilt bias against transience and in favour of its own (purportedly necessary) fictions of permanence. Culture battles to establish nouns, stable unchanging objects and clear-cut authoritative meanings – but in doing so it creates many factitious philosophical difficulties, for the more we are trained to think and operate in terms of stable and permanent things and qualities, the harder we find it to think time, change and events. And the more culture teaches us to associate value with the enduring and the unchanging, the more we will suffer from soul-sickness. For we know in our hearts that our whole being is temporality. We are not merely in time; we just are the time of our lives. We exactly coincide with our own transience. A person is fleeting, *of course* – which means that in so far as culture devalorizes the temporal and the transient, it utterly devalues *us*, and we fall sick. When it postulates a God who is an eternal person, a perfect, absolutely self-identical, infinite spiritual substance, culture is in a strange way deifying and pushing to the limit its own work of fictioning personal identity and timeless value. But a price must be paid: we find that we are alienated from time and transience, and therefore from ourselves. We are set aspiring after what we can never be, a destructive plight to be in.

The cultural fiction of substantiality has been so strong in the West that our traditional formal logic remained tenseless until modern times. Our philosophy, at least before Hegel, was very cautious about engaging with time, the philosophy of history and the history of ideas. In the East, however, the history has been rather different. The Sanskrit term *svabhavā* from *sva* (self) and *bhavā* (being), is variously translated own-being, self-existence, independent existence and so on. It is pretty close in meaning to the Western term substance. And, in the East, it is acknowledged that language and culture do indeed appear to conjure up a world of stable finite substances. But in Mahjayana Buddhism, and in some other traditions too, it is recognized that this is a harmful illusion from which we need to be cured. In reality, everything is empty (*survam shūnyam*). Both our thought-processes and external phenomena lack any permanent substrate or *svabhāva*. All realistic notions of the self, other selves, substances and being are mere constructs (*prajñapati*). And, what is perhaps hardest for your average Westerner to get into his noddle, an education in non-realism is the path to religious liberation. Substance is the work of the Devil, an evil and alienating idea.

Our anti-temporal illusions are very strange, and yet they continue very powerful. Consider the act of reading in which you are presently engaged. There are around forty lines on this page. Most people read a line in three sections, the area of the retina with sharp focus being so very narrow. You read a page a minute. So your eyes flick on to the next little section of print every half-second or so. As you read, meaning flows in time. It is produced, constructed, modified and slips away continuously. Meaning *itself*, therefore is samsāra, flowing temporal process. Which means that everything is temporal. Time-being, being-time. Time is not an external framework, or notion, or whatever. Time is the way everything is. It is outsideless.

That means that in order to be cured of our world-woe we need to give up our ugly, sinful and faithless desire for realistic metaphysics and religious belief. For too long we have tended to take the quasi-fundamentalist view that the way to salvation is to hold on, when the truth is that we must let go. We should embrace the Void – that is, accept transience, and let time be. We have had an ethic of trying to stop the clock and save our selves. The result was inordinate anxiety. We have as yet scarcely tried the alternative, an ethic of completely identifying ourselves with our own temporal procession, our time-being. An ethic of expression and self-giving. Rather hesitantly, we have attributed to God a Pentecostal self-outpouring as Spirit into time and multiplicity. But we so far have been a little reluctant to embrace a similar ethic for ourselves.

(iv) A word in time

It must have become clear by now that there is at least a close analogy between the various charges that people bring against life in general, and the charges they bring against language. Language is not just temporal, but temporizing. It is shifting, ambiguous, evasive and always open to various interpretations. Language won't play straight. It is never wholly with you. It gives, and at the same time it is also taking away. As it moves along it is always looking back and adding nuances to meanings that have already gone, while simultaneously anticipating and preparing for things that are yet to come. Linguistic meaning is distributed over time and is never simply given to us, straightforwardly and all at once. Besides, it always has a contrary undercurrent: every negation seems also to hint at the corresponding affirmation even as it purports to exclude it, and vice versa. Why? Because we always ask ourselves why some statement is being made, and guess that perhaps it is being put forward in order to rebut its contradictory – which is thereby insinuated. It was in this spirit that, at the height of one of those great British sex scandals, a well-known newspaper ran the headline 'Duke of ——— not involved', thus letting us know that according to its information, he was.

These contrary undercurrents that are always present mean that language is always a tease. Often there is no objective sign of the presence of irony or *double entendre*, and our detection of it makes us into fellow-conspirators. Language is a slippery medium that will not let us get it satisfactorily pinned down, and is too tricky to co-operate with us in pinning anything else down. As rueful lawmakers know, definitions can somehow never be made quite definite enough. There is no language without loopholes. Language insists on leaving all truths, all meanings and all values a little up in the air, not quite fully determined and therefore always open to revision, qualification and reinterpretation. Language, infuriatingly, won't keep still and will not close any question. Nothing is finally fixed. Everything comes forward – and then, suddenly, seems to be backing away again. Adapting his notorious saying about truth, Nietzsche would surely conclude that 'Language is a woman'.[13]

It is a deplorable saying, no doubt. But it makes a point that does not have to be read in a sexist way. What happens is that the other human being who is one's close partner, companion, colleague and helpmeet always tends to be seen as a symbol of life itself. A familiar psychological mechanism leads us to see the spouse or the mate as embodying everything we are stuck with, and must learn to rub along with. A woman says in exasperation, 'Men!', as people say, 'That's life', meaning that this is what I am up against, this what I have to cope with. In comedy a great many different relationships can be seen as having this universal quality: big man and little man, maid and mistress, master and man, husband and wife. For each of the pair, unequal though they perhaps are, the other somehow symbolizes everything that is perennially frustrating about the human condition, about life – or about language itself. Since historically men have ensured that they themselves do most of the talking, they have very often presented their complaint about the unsatisfactoriness of life and language in the form of an expostulation about 'woman'. But that is an historical accident. Nowadays we are as likely to hear women answering back in kind. So sexism is not the issue: what we are pointing out is the way a certain cosmic dissatisfaction with life's elusiveness and unmanageability is also a complaint about language and about our dealings with others. And the paradox we are pointing out is this: if our life-woes boil down to woes about language, and if language is outsidelessly all that we have got, how can we even frame our complaint without a certain absurdity? If we are so immersed in language that we can think only in language, then we cannot in fact imagine any other way that things might be. So what are we complaining about?

Let's press the point further, trying to get straight the reasons why things cannot be got quite straight. The basic conditions of life that we are complaining about are time and loss, the fact that no meaning, no truth and no value ever becomes fully rounded-off, perfected, closed and sealed for ever. Life's systematic non-closure, imperfection and transience; that is what we are complaining about. Everything is ambiguous, fickle, unfinished and slipping away out of our grasp. In our own unfinalized linear time death is the chief symbol of the way everything is eventually lost and left unfinished. And this general unsatisfactoriness of life, its refusal ever to deliver completely, is precisely mirrored in the general unsatisfactoriness of language, which turns out to have all the same faults.

Nor is the analogy between life and language an accident – not, at least, on our view. For language actually produces time, and is the medium in which we think and act. Language, that is, actually produces our human life. It produces all meanings and truths and values. So it is scarcely surprising that life should have all the faults that language has. Because we deal with each other and are real to each other only in the language in which we communicate with each other, the other person must appear to us to have all the faults that language has, and life itself must appear to have all the faults of language. If language is always sliding, temporal, ambiguous and never quite completes its delivery of anything, then the other person is going to seem like that and life itself is going to seem like that. Which raises a question about how our complaint can ever get off the ground. If the medium in which we must voice our complaint is responsible for generating the very conditions about which we complain, isn't our complaint oddly self-refuting?

To have any real therapeutic effect, we no doubt need to do more than merely point out the paradox. We must patiently show people, and persuade ourselves too, that language is what it is, and therefore life is what it is; and that we are so completely immersed in life-and-language that we cannot in fact spell out any other way that things might have been for us. Anti-philosophy and anti-theology may thus silence our complaints and reconcile us to life by continually renewing the profound and difficult insight that our life is outsideless. There is nowhere to utter the complaint from.

On this view, the work of redemption does not hike us out of this world, but instead keeps returning us into it with new eyes. In the past both philosophy and religion have very often tried to put things right for us by postulating a world better and more satisfactory than this one. Today, we need to reverse all that. Instead of leading people out of this world towards a better world beyond, we need so to demonstrate the absurdity of all attempts to transcend language that we remove any basis for dissatisfaction with this world. Thus we save the world – by saving it from all invidious comparisons with supposedly better worlds elsewhere. We show that there's no sense in trying to describe in language a world that is free from the limitations that any language-invoked world must have.

For example, it is claimed that Heaven is timeless. It is made of gold and precious stones, which are incorruptible. In Heaven there is no distinction between things open and things kept secret, nor between things still in process and things finished and perfected. In Heaven all truth is published, all meanings are stable, and all values are permanently conserved. It is a world of unalloyed bliss, rounded-off, completed and – as the Bible puts it – sealed for eternity.

Unfortunately, thus to describe heaven in words is to bring it within the realm of language and time, rather as the paintings of it by Fra Angelico and Jan Van Eyck cannot help but make Heaven medieval. And when it is thus made subject to time, and we start trying to imagine our life there, Heaven must begin to sound boring. Boredom is a time-dependent state.

So religion's next move is to try to set the religious object or goal firmly beyond language and time. This requires that language be used, not to describe it, but to fence it about with protective negations and paradoxes. The treatment of God in mystical writings and in the classical negative theology is a highly-developed example of this, but is perhaps over-familiar. An alternative example, which is if anything even more subtle and therapeutic in its design, is the Buddhist language about nirvana. I shall pursue this example in the hope of demonstrating that the harder we press the argument, the more nirvana vanishes. In the end, the quest for a world beyond language can only return us into language. The true liberation is to come back to your starting point. God becomes human, heaven becomes earth, nirvana becomes a way of saying yes, now. That, that, *that* is what our religious myths are telling us, and nothing else.

The opening moves in talk of nirvana are strongly negative in tone. It is the cessation of desire. The saint who has achieved it has gone out like a light. After his thirst or craving has stopped, the five aggregrates (roughly, the constituents of personality) may continue to move, just as a potter's wheel may go on turning for a while after the potter's hand has been removed. But then they fall still. This is parinirvana, nirvana with nothing remaining. In the *Vissudhi Magga*, Buddhaghosa puts it vividly:

> Here suffering exists, but no sufferer is found;
> The deed is, but no doer of the deed is there;
> Nirvana is, but not the man who enters it;
> The Path is, but no traveller on it is seen.[14]

So that is straight extinction – isn't it? The saint has simply gone. He or she is annihilated and freed from the miseries of existence and rebirth. So it may seem; but the Buddha will not confirm this, and in any case, if nirvana were simply extinction how could it be described as a blissful condition? All we get in reply to our questions is the familiar fourfold negation. Metaphysical queries about what may lie beyond the world of space and time, and whether the individual in any case survives death, cannot be appropriately answered either with a Yes, or a No, or with both a Yes and a No, or with neither a Yes nor a No.

So the question of nirvana is left undetermined. Inevitably, though, the commentators have not been content to leave it at that. They have four main lines of interpretation of the Buddha's reasons for not giving a direct answer.

The pragmatic interpretation says that the Buddha will not give a direct answer because for him practice gives the only access to the sort of truth that saves. It is religiously better to leave the metaphysical questions undetermined. They are a distraction. People argue about them forever. Even when given the right answers, people still aren't content. We don't need to have the metaphysical questions answered before we can begin to walk along the Path, and indeed a pure and non-theorized practice of religion just for its own sake is religiously superior, anyway, because it is more disinterested. If practice is put first, everything else will take care of itself.

Taking the same line of argument further, the therapeutic interpretation says that by walking along the Buddhist way we will become cured of the life-woe that troubles us. We will be answered ambulando, by being cured of the disorder that made us ask the question in the first place. For by asking about life after death we showed that we were dissatisfied with this life. This pathological state of dissatisfaction with life will remain with us if we are told that there is a life after death, and it will remain with us if we are told that there isn't. A straight answer is therefore not in fact a helpful response to the question. The Buddha must instead arrange a cure. He does this by shutting off all routes to a theoretical answer, and instead teaching us a way of life that will cure the craving or 'thirst' that was causing our woes. This therapy gets rid of the sickness. And indeed, no good therapist gets into an argument with a patient: instead, he seeks to find a response to the patient that will speed the patient's cure. As everyone knows, all the great founding teachers, Socrates, the Buddha and Jesus were talkers and therapists, not writers and dogmatists.

The linguistic interpretation says that if religion is to deliver us from the world of time and language it clearly cannot attempt to describe the transcendent object or state to which it wants to lead us. Instead it must use negation, paradox and other devices that show rather than say. It must point, but without pointing in any particular direction. Words like above, beyond and outside all invoke the very spatiality from which religion is trying to release us. All of which shows that God, nirvana and suchlike can be neither described nor pointed to. The only remaining option is to resort to negations, paradoxes, silence and so forth. The Buddhist sutras are written in a very clear style, which has the effect of highlighting their sudden lapse into nonsense over nirvana. It makes us think that this must surely be *significant* nonsense.

However, this position doesn't really differ from a simple recommendation to practice religion. If nirvana really is radically indescribable, it collapses into practice through failure to get the distinction between practice and enlightenment, this world and the next, off the ground. So Nāgārjuna and Dōgen offer a non-dualist interpretation. The founding binary distinctions of speculative religious thought cannot get themselves made. You cannot draw the line between what can be said and what cannot be said. You cannot distinguish between the Path and the Goal, this world and the world above, here and there. The young

Wittgenstein thought it could be done by distinguishing between saying and showing and by a technique of indirect communication, but found himself forced to give up the idea. Similarly, Nāgārjuna says that there is only one world: nirvana and samsara (the cycles of birth and death) are the same. They cannot be differentiated from each other. Dōgen adds that practice is enlightenment. Since we cannot make the Here/There distinction, we've got to believe that Here is There and There is Here, already. In several distinct senses, ceaseless practice is all there is here.

Very fine; but we cannot be content to leave it at that. In so far as Nāgārjuna and Dōgen are still ascetics, trying somehow to escape from bondage to time and the passions, they are still slightly dualistic and are still holding back a little from life. They are not quite going the whole way. They don't expressly affirm the Six Truths.

In particular – and I've made this complaint about Buddhism before – they fail to affirm the deep and beautiful truth of outsidelessness. They hang on to some sort of ghost of the idea that there is a silent space somewhere outside time, language and the passions. While they cling to this residuum of the ascetical outlook, they are not yet saying a full religious Yes to time, the passions, language and death. And *that's* what we must do. The argument is that because we are completely immersed in language, it is absurd to suppose that we can somehow think ourselves or work our way out of it. There can be no other Way to salvation except by saying Yes to time, language, the passions and death – in short, to just about everything that our religions hitherto have been in flight from.

This argument at last begins to detach us from Buddhism, from which we have learned so much. Now we are turning towards radical Christian humanism. I say that only a full acceptance of our linguisticality can finally liberate us from illusions and free us to become expressive, creative, value-making, communicative, plural selves. Friends sometimes tell me that they would find my ideas easier to swallow if it weren't for the anti-realism and the wearisome harping on language. But unless language is put first, there will be no final deliverance from otherworldly illusions, and therefore no gospel. The primacy of language means that I must be content not to be a substantial and metaphysical self but only a protean, temporal and languagey self. This 'theatrical' self that exists only in its own communicative expression is the only sort of self that is going to be content to 'die daily'. Religion, now, is to be content to pour yourself out unreservedly into the living of your own mortal life. In Christianity we say, 'God was content so to give himself up or hand himself over. We too should be content to expend ourselves.' This is salvation. It is the truth, all of it.

(v)   Curing what?

Our talk of a cure, you may object, is not merely metaphorical. It's mythical. It sets up a contrast between the way we are now and a primal founding state of health and well-being that we allegedly need to get back to. That's a mythical pattern of thought, if ever there was one. It invokes a Golden Age, an original perfection by contrast with which the whole of our present existence looks blighted. But the very idea of such a Golden Age is quite unhistorical, and rather uselessly discouraging. It is also very woolly and ill thought-out. Even in everyday medicine the notion of health is notoriously vague, and influenced by current fashions and expectations. There is no such thing as perfect bodily health. Mental health, too, is only a metaphor[15] and always relative to local cultural norms. As for a healthy human-condition-as-such, or view thereof, what could that be?

In reply, I'm not trying to get back to any lost paradise. In fact, as you'll see, the movement is going to be in the reverse direction, from dreams of paradise back into the midst of life. I am saying rather in the style of the later Wittgenstein, that we have been troubled and distracted by a misleading picture. The noun-verb distinction in the language has long been suggesting to us that the being of a thing can be distinguished from its temporality, and in particular that a human person can be distinguished from the unfolding temporal process of her living. This is a mistake, but it has been a very influential one, for it is upon this basis that, both in the East and the West, the existence of the self or soul has for so long been debated as a topic in metaphysics. Perhaps, indeed, it was the noun-verb distinction that first gave rise to metaphysics. At any rate, the West, following Plato and Augustine, very often said: 'Yes, we are selves indeed, out of time. We are immortal rational souls. Just now we are embodied, and we have a human historical life to live. The way we live it will determine our eternal destiny.' This manner of speaking certainly suggests a clear distinction between a metaphysical self and the historical life that is its short-term but all-important task. Because our eternal destiny was at stake in every fleeting moment and every decision of our life in time, the West developed very lively and dramatic traditions of biography and autobiography. By contrast, the East Asian tradition of Buddhism said simply that there is no metaphysical self, only a collection of processes. That is correct so far as it goes, but unfortunately Buddhism also lacked a strong conception of linear historical time. It therefore had no motive to develop any vigorous traditions of biography or spiritual autobiography. The self never became properly activated, either metaphysically or historically.

I suggest that neither the typical Western nor the typical Eastern view gets the relation of selfhood to time right. Neither understands the ontology correctly, because neither recognizes that a person is like a role in a play. Personality is made of communicative behaviours, and is built up over time. Consider the case of someone close to you. What is he to you? A still photograph is not he; it can do no more than remind you of him. To you, he is your still-growing and changing interpretation of his role in your relations with him, accumulated over years maybe. He's something like a literary construction. He's made of signs, and both he and your view of him are essentially temporal. He's a little elusive even to himself, because there are so many different perceptions of him. All are changeable, and none is right. But that's life; that's language. We are ambiguous. We are clusters of possible interpretations, and there is no one final truth about any of us. Since we are outsidelessly always in time, finality is never reached, not even about the dead.

Check out your own life. There is a range of possible and plausible readings of you and what you are up to, some more favourable and some less so. If there is no objective truth about you, what are you struggling for? Answer: like us all, you're trying to make life, make love and make work. And you are doubtless trying to tilt the balance of the argument towards the more favourable rather than the less favourable versions of what you're up to and what you amount to. You're trying to bear witness to certain values; you're trying to make your contribution. Thus the self as such doesn't matter very much (which is why we can cheerfully take a reductionist view of it), but what does matter and is interesting is the story of its endeavour to bear witness to and give itself to something other than itself. The question about the self, then, is going to come out like this: your life will have been worth living if one day a decently-plausible story can be told about how you gave it for a cause.

So the no-self doctrine means this: after we have dissolved away certain illusions that were created by language, I realize that I can no longer say metaphysically that I am a self, nor even that I have a life. No: I am exactly the time of my life. Being and temporality coincide. You can't slip even so much as a knife-blade between them. You are your life, and your life is the story of your life. Or rather, it's the cluster of possible stories of your life. And the story is not over yet. There may still be some twists in the plot. Your life will have value if it bears witness to value; that is, your life will have been worth living if its story can plausibly be told as the story of a dedicated life.

I am admitting all along that there is no objective measure of saintliness. There are only stories, some more and some less plausible, about lives. Is this fatal to my account? Does it matter that after the dissolution of reality and value into a flux of narratives and interpretations, no objective measure of virtue or holiness remains? No, I don't think it does matter, and in fact we are very traditional on this point. Under the older theistic scheme of thought you were similarly warned not to bank on your own valuation of your achievements or your virtues. The only verdict upon you that counted in the end was God's, and you could not know what that might turn out to be. Meanwhile, your own self-estimation was not to be relied upon. So the older scheme of thought, just as much as the new, warned you to be wary of your own valuations and self-estimation. It told you not to put your trust in your achievements, nor to be too sure of your own story about your life. Under the old scheme of thought God might suddenly appear and utterly confound your version of your life. You should repent, and stop trusting in yourself. And under the new scheme of thought, I say too that we should give up the idea that we have any power to make morally-secure selves of ourselves. A person is only a story, and stories are inherently ambiguous. Caesar, thou art mortal: the man who seems a fine fellow to himself looks a conceited prick to others. Which point of view is right? Both, maybe. Meanwhile, the best sort of life to live is an uncompromisingly dedicated life, that is, a life in which I don't even try to make a self of myself, but instead give myself.

The true cure, and the true liberation then, is to be freed from the myth of metaphysical selfhood, but still to believe in linear time. This returns me into the time of my life. When I am liberated into exact coincidence with my own lifetime there is no longer any alienation between time and being.

For our new religion, the true liberation is no longer liberation from this world and this life of ours, but liberation into it. And the good life is not a life in which I try to make something supra-temporal of myself, but a life freely given, lived-towards-death, dedicated and poured out. Every ethic enacts a metaphysic, so our no-self metaphysics will be dramatized in a no-self ethics. There being no self, we must live selflessly. I am not an immortal soul but only a *dramatis persona*, so I must play my part. Paradoxically, when we are freed from the illusions of metaphysical selfhood, and fully accept that our being and our expressive living are one and the same, we find we are strengthened and made able to create. We do it, because we have to. Boris Pasternak is reported to have said that an artist must look death in the face every morning. That's dead right – and, brothers and sisters, please meditate at length upon that beautiful and poetical use of dead to mean exact, precise and perfect. It describes a Zen quality that our words and deeds can achieve if we stop running away from temporality, secondariness and death, and begin instead to live in and for the baseless moment and movement of life.

Die with Christ, yes. But don't die out of life. Die back into life, by giving up any distinction between noun and verb, or existence and time. Say yes to outsidelessness, truthlessness, secondariness and mortality. Become a saint of imperfection, for the time being – and *then* you can become creative.

8

HOW WE SHOULD LIVE

(i) Freedom

We need to learn and learn from Buddhist spirituality, but I am also saying that there comes a moment at which we must diverge from it. With the turn to ethics, the reason for this becomes clearer. Buddhist spirituality seems to point to an ethic of non-violence, temperance, universal dispassionate compassion, cool-ness and calmness of soul, and receptive aesthetic contemplation of the transient. It sounds like an ethic for the retired, and indeed there is a certain tendency in Japan to associate the wisdom of Buddhism with extreme old age and the dead.

No harm in that. We in the West sorely need a spirituality and an ethic for the closing months or years of life, and we would do well to look to East Asian Buddhism for assistance in developing it. But so far as the production of human life as a whole is concerned, we have found ourselves laying more emphasis than Buddhism does upon language, linear time and narrativity, and therefore upon life as like theatre. In the theatre, the script we are given produces reality by casting us in various roles. As we act in these roles, the story develops through our emotional engagement with each other and our battles against each other. And although the dramatist in the case of a play, or culture in the case of life in general, may have scripted our roles very tightly, still, the nature of language is such as to compel us to produce our own personal interpretations of the parts we've been given to play. However tight the scripting, there is always need for an exercise of creative freedom in the production of one's own performance. In fact, we become individual persons only in and through the way we put a bit of personal spin upon our playing of the parts we have been given.

Don't misunderstand me. I am not proposing by the theatrical metaphor any return to a dualistic view of the self. There is no intention to reinstate the old contrast between an independent human subject and the various social roles and masks that it assumes. On the contrary, if *all* the world's a stage then we are never not acting, and the script is never not being interpreted. The liberating point of the theatrical metaphor is not that there is a real self behind the performance we give, but simply that we cannot be railroaded. Determinism is a non-issue. Interpretations of the script are and are going to remain endlessly varied and variable. A one-level self immersed in its own performance can still think of itself as freely giving the show it puts on.

We turn from Buddhism, as we turn also from Platonism, because they have always objected to and have tried to abstract away from the theatricality of life. They have never really been able to stomach the various ambiguities and vulnerabilities that we are caught up in by our role-playing and our emotional battles with each other. But I am saying that we need an ethic that accepts the theatricality of life, and I have called this ethic active non-realism. It is a non-realist ethical stance that asks us to recognize that if we are to be agents we must be actors. Culture assigns to us roles, a script and certain stage props. Very well, we must make the most of these resources and try to put on a good show, producing our own lives as performance art. And it won't be a good show unless we really commit ourselves to our parts and make something of them.

The Judaeo-Christian religious traditions are full of narrative and mythic drama, a good deal of which is expressly proposed to us as an outline script to be acted out in our lives. But the theatrical metaphors remain rather undeveloped, because we have preferred to opt instead for moralities of rational self-control and conformity to law.[1]

Nevertheless, at least some anticipations of the ethics of active

non-realism are to be found in the ethical teaching attributed to
Jesus. He says, for example: 'The sabbath was made for man, not
man for the sabbath.'[2] I interpret that to mean: 'Treat the moral
tradition that has come down to you not as a cage but as a tool,
not as a rigid Law but as an acting script, to be interpreted as may
seem appropriate. Don't be like the scribes and the canon lawyers.
Make truth your own, and make your own truth.'

Again, consider the saying: 'Take no thought for the morrow.'[3]
I take this to be saying a bit more than just, Make no plans. It
says: 'Don't lock yourself in, don't mortgage all your freedom
and become the prisoner of your commitments. Don't sell out to
ulteriorism or long-termism. Keep a bit of the freedom to make
up your own life as you go along.'

Again: 'The Kingdom of God is within, or among, you.'[4] This
says: 'Just in the energy of language itself, running through you
and pouring out of you, there is a never-exhausted supply of new
metaphors, new feelings and new meanings. Make contact with
that source of creativity and life-energy, and live from it. Trust
it.'

Finally, 'Resist not evil',[5] which means: 'Beware of those who
always seek to divide up the world into good and evil camps.
Beware of dualistic ways of thinking. Beware of those who strive
to impose law and order upon others. Such people live by the
sword, but your way should be different from theirs.'

So I claim that active non-realism is implied in Jesus teaching
– or at least, may be read there. The Kingdom of God is a world
in which free human beings continually make and remake the
world they live in and the values they live by. It is a world of
freedom, freedom to make the rules and not just freedom to obey
them. But it has to be said that we in the West have so far shown
little enthusiasm for moral freedom as the non-realist conceives
it. We have been preoccupied with the problem of social control,
and have put all the stress on the close regulation of life by the
Law rather than upon the creative freedom to reinterpret the Law
and bend it to suit ourselves. We have been more interested in
developing dogmas about Jesus and using them as tools of power,

than in making something of his teaching. Christianity neutralized Jesus by turning him into everything that he warned people against.

The philosophical tradition has taken a similar line. Until very recently active non-realism in ethics was described as 'emotivism' or 'subjectivism', and represented as being a distinctly immoral view to hold. To this day many people still equate moral serious-ness with moral realism, the belief that we need to posit something unchanging out there which provides morality with a rock-solid and extrinsic guarantee or foundation. The doctrine that we create and must create our own values was associated with Nietzsche and Sartre, and was viewed as dangerous and excessive. People thought that if it became widely prevalent it would lead to social disaster.

The result of this has been that to a surprising degree we still instinctively represent moral goodness and virtue as consisting in conformity to some sort of objective standard. It might be pictured as a Law, a rule, a model, a principle, a norm, a value or an essence. The vocabulary is large and extremely vague. Never mind: the underlying theme is clear enough. We equate morality with moral subjection to something out there, and don't yet think in terms of creative freedom and innovation.

I am saying, however, that we should see religion and morality not in terms of conformity to external norms, but in terms of theme and variations, text and interpretations. We should be looking for reinterpretation, improvisation and innovation *against* received norms, rather than a state of docile subjection *to* received norms. The norm should be a state of permanent revolution against the norm; the tradition should be anti-tra-dition. Yes, of course, the tradition prescribes a vocabulary, roles, language-games and so on: but the theatrical metaphor reminds us that however much has been prescribed, your acting of the part assigned to you will also be your own personal reading of it.

This conception of freedom is a great advance upon the older debate, which looked for ways of fitting a bit of pure spirit-freedom into a mechanistic universe. The outlook that resulted was unavoidably, but unsuccessfully, dualistic. People believed in the existence of a machine universe out there, all of whose motions strictly conformed to the laws of mathematical physics. God was not ruled out. It could be held that he had made the machine and set it moving, and he might be thought of as having reason occasionally to interfere with it. God, then, could be free: what about us? Unlike God we have bodies, which are parts of the machine and are subject to its laws, but it seemed that freedom of thought and of moral decision might yet be salvaged if they were located in a parallel mental world. So people were led to postulate mental-event/physical-event dualism and parallelism. God precalculates everything and keeps the two worlds in step. But nobody could say clearly how a chain of occurrences in the mental world could be an expression of freedom and rationality, while the precisely-corresponding chain of brain-events in the world of matter could express nothing but the principles of mechanistic determinism. Mind-matter dualism was quite vivid as an image of the problem of freedom of action in a mechanistic universe; but it did nothing to resolve the contradiction that it portrayed.

The turn to language eases matters. The clockwork universe becomes just a metaphor. It is associated with a set of mathematical rules and procedures by following which we can regularly get our sums right or very, very nearly so. But a mathematical 'model' isn't really a *model* at all, and the fact that certain mathematical procedures are useful and work well in practice doesn't by itself give us any information about the objective existence or the character of a supposed universe out there. The physical realism of the older outlook was indeed nothing but an illusion produced by a lot of metaphors. Thus, talk of 'applied' mathematics seems to whisper to us that mathematical rules are applied to or laid over reality as railway tracks are laid over Yorkshire. Talk of 'natural laws' suggests that Nature obeys physical laws pretty much as people obey the civil law within the state. And similar considerations apply to talk about models and machines. The hard-edged mechanistic universe was never more than a picture that for a while held many people's imaginations captive. Now, happily, we are hearing very much less about it. People are readier to acknowledge that scientific vocabularies are metaphorical, highly angled and selective, and open to reinterpretation. Descriptive meaning cannot be pinned down strictly in the way that mechanistic determinism required. On the contrary, the history of science shows that over the generations cultural change can curiously alter the aspect of even the most familiar and clearly-specified scientific theory. Science is cultural, and more subtly flavoured by its own period than the practitioners care to acknowledge.

As everything is absorbed into the general movement of language, culture and history, so the world becomes a continuum. We cannot any longer draw clear lines of separation between matter and mind, objectivity and subjectivity, nature and culture.

So instead of the old physical-determinism-versus-mental-freedom cosmology we now have a new picture. We contrast the admittedly-powerful cultural programming of all our life and language with the various ways in which, just by acting, we must each of us realize and express our own individuality. The general model will be the way a concert pianist dutifully plays all the notes written for her in the score – and yet in doing so also gives us a new and personal interpretation of the piece. Notice the paradox: as compared with Asian music, Western music is *both* more highly pre-scribed *and* gives more scope for individual expression.

That's freedom. The cultural forms with which you have been programmed cannot help but permit you to impress something that is uniquely your own upon the performance that they require you to give. Indeed, if the cultural forms are lively and of high quality, they will actually facilitate the performer's individual expression.

How then can some standard cultural form function as a means to individual self-expression for a whole variety of different performers? To answer this question we need first to shake off the tyranny of literalism. Literalism says roughly, language is transparent, words conduct us directly to the things and thoughts they stand for, and a text has just one literal meaning, namely all the states of affairs and events that it describes. But shake off this barbarous view of language, become more aware of what language's own properties are and of all the tricks and games that can be played with it – become, in short, a non-realist about language – and everything is changed. We start to see the express-ive and emancipatory possibilities of language. We see that no régime can ever completely control language. Artists and writers will always find loopholes in metaphor, irony, *double entendre* and so forth. No tyrant is proof against mockery.

The religious implications are clear. We have inherited the remains of a religion of dogmatic definitions, and canonical forms for almost everything. It was all about power – masculine power, of course – and subjection to power. To find freedom, people in the past were obliged to find ways of outwitting it or escaping it. Today they can simply disregard it, and are doing so. Nor should we seek to recreate the same sort of system. Instead, it would be better to develop a religion of subversion and creativity, so that people can find new ways of expressing their individuality in our highly-managed societies. And in the long run we want to see people become the conscious and trained makers of meanings and values, and the artists of their own lives.

(ii) Playing up

Under the traditional Western scheme of thought human freedom, whether you had much of it or little, was exercised *vis à vis* the will of God or the laws of nature. Under the newer scheme of thought our freedom, whether much or little, has to be exercised *vis à vis* the structures that have been imposed upon us by culture and through which we must live. This shift makes a significant difference to ethics. For culture is not content merely to provide us with language (vocabulary, grammar, syntax and value-flavours annexed to words), and then leave us to get on with it. No: culture does a lot more than that. It structures the temporal movement or process of life, classifying and stereotyping all our diverse activities so as to give them each its own distinct formal, ritualized and gamelike character.

This is not an easy thing to see. But most people will have noticed how words cut up the world of experience into discrete blocks. Nouns in particular impose a classification upon the world, very much as newspapers must represent everything they report in clichés and stereotypes so as to make it intelligible. That is how we function. Words and ideas have to be general. And culture treats our life in time in the same way, breaking up the temporal continuum into the various units of time and the feasts and fasts and seasons, and also breaking up our various activities into ritualized games, each with its own style and rules. All our daily doings, activities, exchanges and leisure pursuits thus get pushed into slots and conventionalized, so that they can the more easily be recognized and differentiated from each other. It is decreed that there is a right and a wrong way to do everything, which effectively means that for each activity there is a socially-recognized proper place, time, dress, set of linguistic forms and manner in which to do it. If you follow the right form other people will be able to tell what you are up to, and can then behave appropriately. So the ritualization of behaviours has a cognitive and practical function. Just as the common nouns create a simplified, spread-out realm of discrete objects in order to give us a discussible and navigable common world to know and move around in, so the ritualization of all human activities makes social co-operation possible.

We all of us demand ritualization. When our gamelike activities take place in due form we feel comfortable and reassured. We know what's happening. Conversely, any departure from standard form, whether accidental or deliberate, causes acute general embarrassment and discomfort. This morning, perhaps, you have already assumed successively the roles of spouse, parent, newspaper reader, motorist, worker, customer and so on. You have dealt in different ways with banter, telephone calls, clients, correspondence, inspectors, complaints and disputes. In the course of these varied activities you will have played many different roles. Having good social skills means being able to play each game correctly without getting hold of the wrong end of the stick. You have to be able to change gear and move smoothly into each new game as occasion demands. You must know the ropes and make people feel that you're with them. If you can do all that, if you can as people say put on a polished performance, playing always bang in the middle of the role assigned to you in whatever game is being played, then you'll undoubtedly go far in the world. Those who win the game are those who play it the most smoothly and easily.

I am saying, then, that even in the most advanced bourgeois societies, where people pride themselves on their informality and personal authenticity, the daily activities of life remain almost as highly ritualized as in the most archaic societies. There has been a long tradition in Europe of debate between those who view human society as a market and those who view it as theatre.[6] Both models are very powerful and illuminating, but just for the present the theatrical metaphor is uppermost.

However, even more significant is the fact that almost the whole of our philosophical and religious tradition has been highly anti-theatrical,[7] and for long resisted the development of our modern concept of culture. Somehow we didn't want to know that in order to make social life possible at all, culture must prescribe in great detail our vision of the world, our values, and due forms for all the manifold activities of daily life. Through language and by regulating our practices, culture gives us both our common life-world and our common way of life.

Before quite modern times, this obvious insight was somehow withheld. All that people had by way of a concept of culture was the notion of local manners and customs, which were clearly distinguished from serious matters of faith and morals, and reduced to the level of local curiosities reported by travellers. Culture was not really allowed to contaminate serious matters of rationality, religion and ethics. In these areas we pictured ourselves as naked spirits under God's heaven, unconstrained by history, language and our social relations. Our morality and religion seemed to us to be just plain cosmic facts that had been vouchsafed to us from above, and therefore had not suffered any contamination by the horizontal. Indeed, these cosmic facts had created society, and not the other way round.

So our religion and philosophy were highly ideological, in that they systematically deceived us about their own true status. They bumped up their own authority by pretending to have come down from heaven, which meant that they needed to conceal their earthly parentage. Accordingly, the whole realm of the social was largely kept out of sight until the nineteenth century.

There was good reason for this. We very much did *not* want to know that all our traditional moral and religious convictions are simply contingent, historically-evolved and changeable human customs. They do a good job in that they co-ordinate our social behaviour, but they are sanctified only by long habit. And they are by no means immutable. Indeed, like all usages, they are slowly evolving all the time.

It is still not easy to grasp the full implications of all this. I am puzzled when I consider that society prescribes both the vocabulary I must live in and the due forms of all my daily activities. That sounds like a very severe restriction of freedom. But the rules that limit our freedom are after all nothing but historically-evolved and still-evolving communal habits. So just how tightly *are* we constrained?

The sense of puzzlement arises because our historic ways of thinking no longer work. We have in the past set up the problem of moral and religious freedom in terms of the material-spiritual distinction. Spirit has ready access to unchanging religious and moral truths that come down to it from a higher world, and it looks for such loopholes in physical law as will allow it to put them into practice here below. But the newer point of view requires a different conception of morality and religion. Moral and religious truth will reside, not in some corpus of timeless, and maybe revealed, truths but in whatever personal twist we can give to our acting of the script that society hands to us. Religion and morality become creative and interpretative activities by which we add to and bend a little the traditions we have received.

This makes our action merely relative to conventions, I allow; but consider the following: what makes theatrical action action?[8] The philosophy of theatre is a singularly undeveloped subject, but I suggest that reflection on the problem of theatrical action will show indirectly that the efficacy, not only of speech-acts, but of social action generally, is also only conventional. Our tradition has tried to make our action natural, but it isn't. Only through cultural conventions can human action be framed and understood as such.

How feather-light these considerations make everything seem! I find it hard to accept that truths and values that we should be ready to die for are only 'positive', mere contingent human arrangements. I'm not saying they are non-rational. On the contrary, they need to be for the best. But they'll be so only in *our* eyes. Our judgment on the point will be uncorroborated. Hard. But it is still not easy to take in the really true truth about the human condition, which is that we are in an outsideless language-evoked flux of becoming, a flux which is always at once a coming-to-be and a passing-away. The unbearable lightness of being – our post-Buddhism of the sign, our fictionalism. A world quite unanchored and free-floating, but a world that constrains us because we, poor fools, are lighter still.

Now, historically, religion and philosophy in the West have feared and dreaded this lightness. They have seen it as their task to solidify the world. The defence of realism has been a prime duty. We must strive with all our might to vindicate reason, knowledge and morality, and this can only be done by grounding our knowledge and our values in some objective and enduring Reality. Either they are to be founded in the natural order of the world about us, or they are to be referred to a more Real World beyond space and time. It's either Aristotle or Plato: so people have thought, and in many cases think still.

The end of the old realism and foundationalism, the end in

short of the old illusory dogmatic philosophy and religion, is a great event. It requires us to become genuinely lightfooted, critical and creative at last, both in religion and in morality. Truly creative religion and morality will be perfectly content to operate in a very light world, and indeed the Christian doctrine of redemption always promised that one day we would see people become creators in a fully humanized world. I am delivering that promise, right?

It has to be recognized that the self has changed. It is not a substance any longer, not a spirit, but only a slightly deviant and ironical interpretation. More sprite than spirit.

It sounds, at first, too lightweight to be capable of moving the world. Our social life is still very crude and primitive, constrained by cultural habits to function only in ritualized slots. The slotting, as we have seen, is for the sake of intelligibility: if custom decrees that there's only a small number of discrete things that you *can* be doing, then that'll make it easy for others to distinguish what you are trying to do from what you're not trying to do. So culture has, so far at least, always compelled us to be leaden clichés and to act in clichés in order that our doings may be intelligible to others.

We are still locked into this position. It has produced us. We have and we are only the language and the cultural forms out of which we are made and in which we must express ourselves. Our philosophical and religious traditions used to claim that it was possible for us to step out of all language-games and role-playing and become pure, naked, recollected selves. But this I have denied at length. Life is theatre. In the late Baroque and Rococo, the Catholic religion visibly admits its own theatricality, and makes the crucial acknowledgment that the line separating the real from the fictional is itself a fiction. Private prayer and public worship don't happen in some privileged space outside all games, but are themselves also games that we play. So we should give up the pretence that there is a real self in there behind all the masks we wear and the games we play. No: we are theatrical all the way down. We cannot function, we cannot express ourselves and we don't even exist except within a régime of signs, a game-situation and a cultural tradition.

So we've got to play the game, and we should not look for ways of dropping out of it. But we can play up a little. We need a more literary approach to morality and religion that will show us how we can breathe new life into old texts, and how we can so interpret a role as to send it up.

A feature of the modern West is that people are worried that reality is melting away. They complain about falling standards, collapsing values and decaying truth. Yet if people were genuine realists they would not be thinking that reality, standards, values and truths were the sorts of things that could ever collapse. The vocabulary that people use implies their tacit admission that the old classical palace we inhabit, which we once took for Reality itself, has now been discovered to be a purely human construction. We learnt this in a very simple way: we found it was decaying with age, just as any other human building would decay. That sort of realization is irreversible, because of the paradox implied in attempting to refabricate the confidence that something is not a fabrication.

We are unlikely, then, to be able to re-establish the old plain outdoor and extra-theatrical reality of things. We should not waste time in lamenting the disappearing distinctions between sincerity and play-acting, truth and fiction, reality and illusion. Instead we should get used to living creatively in a very thin world. And we should get used to a new distinction, between the various stereotyped and often unsatisfactory roles that culture gives us to play, and our own efforts to reinterpret them, subvert them, laugh at them and, in the long run, remake them.

Can you imagine a religion that consisted not in a solemnization of the *status quo*, but in a mood of laughter added to life?

(iii) *Living on the brink*

It is very common to hear people say that we should take life as
it comes, live one day at a time, and not waste our strength either
in futile regrets about the past or in anxiety about the future. Yet
the people who say this kind of thing are paying in their pension
contributions and booking engagements in their diaries just like
anyone else, which makes one wonder what their advice amounts
to. Is there nothing more to it than the commendation of an
attitude? Maybe; but if so, then it is an attitude to life that is urged
upon us in a great variety of vocabularies. Charismatic religion
says: 'Don't prepare a speech, because on the spur of the moment
the Spirit will teach you what to say.' Wordsworth advises us to
live by the heart, and many other Romantics say something
similar. Kierkegaard says: 'The Gentiles wear themselves out with
anxiety about the future. The birds of the air and the lilies of the
field live simply in the present moment. But you should live
eternally in the present.'[9] He seems to mean that human existence
is suspended between metaphysical polarities, such as the contrast
between time and eternity, but that we can reconcile or mediate
the oppositions by the way we choose to live. Choose to be
yourself as an individual ethical subject who lives and acts in time,
Kierkegaard tells us, and in that choice relate each moment of
your life to the Eternal. Will one thing: that is eternal life.

I too want to commend short-termism, but not in quite the
usual Western vocabularies. They are too vague and woolly, and
if perchance they do get spelled out a little more clearly they seem
to become objectionable. Charismatic talk about relying upon
ad hoc guidings and inspirations of the Spirit sounds too like
supernaturalism. Romantic talk about relying upon the flow of
natural feelings and instincts is a trifle optimistic, as the Marquis
de Sade has pointed out in quite sufficient detail. In any case, it
takes culture to produce and form our natural feelings and
instincts, and to read them as giving directives. The feelings of the
heart are not pure and original in the way that many of the
Romantics supposed. The classical case is woman. In the nine-

teenth century she was supposed to have 'a woman's heart' which was just full of pure and original guiding feelings and instincts that she should follow, and that men should reverence in her. But the more recent post-World-War-Two insight, following Simone de Beauvoir, is that 'one is not born a woman but *made* a woman.' 'Woman', in the nineteenth-century sense, was a complex cultural creation. All of which strongly suggests that our natural feelings and instincts are by no means such innocent or original guides to spontaneous living as some have claimed. They are cultural imperatives in disguise; and they have needed to disguise themselves precisely because they are highly questionable.

Kierkegaard tells a more complex story.[10] No systematic or scientific philosophy can be an adequate guide to life, he says. The continual coming-to-be of things is not necessitated; it is purely contingent, and therefore not predictable. Besides, life's movement means that it always escapes systematic comprehension. 'Life in time can never be properly understood, just because no moment can acquire the complete stillness needed to orient oneself backwards.' It follows that 'the subjective thinker is not a scientist, he is an artist. Existing is an art. The subjective thinker is aesthetic enough to give his life aesthetic [i.e., immediate, sensuous] content, ethical-enough to regulate it, and dialectical enough to master it in thought.' All of which implies that Kierkegaard's notion of living eternally in the present moment is pretty strenuous. It does involve an affirmation of the transient, indeed; but it also requires a continually renewed choice whereby the transient is referred to eternity. Heavy going, especially in what Kierkegaard calls the 'A'-position, where the old contrasts between finite and infinite, possibility and necessity, and time and eternity, press hard upon the soul. 'Religiousness A' does sound a bit like Hegel's 'unhappy consciousness'. However, the more Christian position, according to Kierkegaard, is 'Religiousness B'. Here the platonic contrasts have receded, and Kierkegaard takes a non-realist view of God. He points out through his pseudonym Climacus that 'Christianity has preached eternity as the future life'. God is 'the possible', the open future before us, and faith is a passionate, trusting commitment to life that propels one forward into an unknowable future bounded by death.

This is still pretty hard work, and although once again I want to claim that Kierkegaard's position is not so very far from mine,[11] the present discussion calls for a somewhat different line of argument.

My general thesis, as you would expect, is that for the sake of our salvation we need to become non-realists. We should think of ourselves as very light and living in a gossamer world, teetering all the time on the brink of nothingness. Radical anti-realism is the way to blessedness. It alone can make us self-less, emptied-out, free and innocently creative. But my version of the doctrine diverges somewhat from Mahayana Buddhism, because I reject (or at any rate take a purely negative view of) what Buddhism calls the truth of the highest meaning. I stay with language and the lower-level 'conventional truth' that language produces, which means that we stay with an ultralight Christian humanism instead of going on to the full Buddhist position.

We make five moves. First, we reject the platonic oppositions. Kierkegaard still felt them acutely. Today, as a matter of simple empirical fact, we no longer feel that way. We just don't any longer articulate our experience of life in terms of the classic contrasts between finite and infinite, possibility and necessity, time and eternity. Secondly, we affirm instead that the world presents itself to us as a continuous flux of purely contingent language-formed experience. The world is always already covered over with our language, our theories, our perspectival views. We never see the world as it is in itself, apart from and prior to our construals of it. It is always packaged in language. The result is that for us who live in time, being presents itself to us in the same way as linguistic meaning does. The real presents itself as a continuous coming-to-be which never quite succeeds in becoming complete and substantial and is always already passing away again. As it comes it is already going. That's the truth of the Buddhist doctrine of 'conditioned co-arising' or 'dependent origination' (*pratītya samutpāda*). Everything is like the Cheshire

Cat's smile – secondary, consequential, relative, reciprocally-conditioning and not really able to exist on its own. Which is how meaning comes to us in sentences; always flowing and relative, never getting to be fully-fixed. So we should be unmetaphysical and hold no position, not even the position that no position is true. Sunyata-sunyata: the doctrine that all things are empty is itself also empty. Our outlook in religion and philosophy needs to be beliefless, fluid, pragmatic, therapeutic. The aim of philosophical thinking and religious practice is to unblock us. We need to become fully open and receptive to the flow of time and meaning. Egoism, anxiety and hate constipate the soul, making us unable either to let life be or to love others. No views, no position, no convictions: tenets only make people self-important and obnoxious.[12]

Thirdly, we do not attempt to go beyond language. Language is outsideless. Attempts to go beyond it must nevertheless remain within it. The point of our radically language-centred philosophy is that it safeguards Christian humanism. So long as we are careful to follow Wittgenstein and remain within language, we will stay with the (admittedly) very light world that language evokes, together with the (again, admittedly) light and provisional feelings, valuations and selfhood that language gives us. So we say a firm yes to time, conventional truth and the human world, ultralight though they are. The only 'truths of the highest meaning' that we recognize are the Six Truths expounded in Chapter 2, and they function only to return us into conventional – that is, human – reality. They are like No Road signs, or limit-concepts.

So, fourthly, we say yes to pure contingency and we live on the brink. We say yes to language, time, the passions and narrative selfhood. When we compare life with a game or a dance we are emphasizing and indeed welcoming its lightness and pointlessness. The besetting sin of much of our traditional Western philosophy and religion was its insistence upon seeking some kind of extrinsic ballast and justification for life. It was supposed that our life needed to be given reality, value and a goal from a point outside it. This was a mistake. We should be attempting the exact opposite.

Religion should be a cure for metaphysics and a joyful celebration of transience.

Fifthly and finally, we say yes to the passions but no to 'clinging'. There is a question here about how the Buddhist critique of craving or clinging is to be understood. Possibly because we look at Buddhism with the eyes of platonism, we tend to hear in Buddhism the same criticisms of the passions that we have already heard from Plato. This may be wrong, and many recent expositors of Buddhism equate 'non-clinging' not with passionlessness but with anti-realism. The clinger is the realist, the person enslaved by objectifying ways of thinking, who seems unable to live without positing unchanging verities out-there and then becoming fixated upon them. Clinging is what the typical realistic Christian thinks of as faith, and I agree with the Buddhists that it should instead be regarded as the opposite of faith. It leads away from salvation.

There is a slight doubt, then, about whether the Mahayana Buddhist philosophers are attacking realism or are attacking the passions. I am not quite sure how we should read them. Perhaps it is up to Buddhists and the Buddhist scholars themselves to decide how they wish to read their own texts. As for us, we seek to combine the humanist tradition which says Yes to the passions, with the mystical tradition which says No to attachment or clinging. A long-established set of metaphors leads us to suspect the passions of being leaden and earthbound. They drag us down, they are injurious to the soul. In tragedy the passions are indeed so portrayed; but in comedy the passions are light. They don't enslave, but exhilarate – and why not?

(iv) The democratic politician

If there is no objective and overarching moral order whose authority is generally acknowledged, then human beings must posit one for themselves. In our large-scale, plural and continuously-changing societies this is no easy task. It calls for a type of person who has antennae very sensitive to the climate of opinion, and the knack of finding words that will successfully explicit and articulate a public consensus that can hold for a while. But this character-type we are imagining is going to have to be very flexible, moving with the tide of opinion and continuously adapting the expressed consensus as times change. A difficult balancing-act has to be performed; you must lead, but you must keep in touch. If you go too far and use language that runs beyond what people will support, then you have become too strong a leader and are accused of being bossy, as happened to the British Prime Minister, Margaret Thatcher, in 1990-91. Her successor John Major was at first welcomed as being much more responsive to public opinion, but soon found himself accused of being too accommo-dating. He was a ditherer, said the critics; he was, they declared, like the cushion that always bears the imprint of the last backside to sit on it. The right balance between leadership and responsive-ness is hard to strike. Nevertheless the sort of person I am describing has to be found, and performs an indispensable moral function. I am talking about the democratic politician, a flexible, light-footed, trendy improviser, and the chief creator and sustainer of the moral order in modern societies.

The entire realist tradition since Plato has denied that values are subject to historical change, and has accordingly despised the politician's manoeuvering. Believing that we can have objective knowledge of an objective order of reality and value, the realist supposes that we therefore can and should live by clear and unchanging principles. The imagery used suggests inflexibility. You don't allow yourself to be blown off-course, but sail straight ahead. You don't adapt your principles to changing times; you merely re-apply them. Principles are to be stuck to. And while this sort of thing is being said, the work of flexible, unprincipled politicians and negotiators will tend to be underrated.[13]

There has, however, always been a different opinion. The world of the early civilizations was chronically balkanized. It was a world of endless political unrest, overheated passions and warring city states. In such circumstances, kings did not in the least want uncompromising men of principle to be their servants. They wanted very polished and self-controlled people, untroubled by strong personal convictions, to serve them as counsellors, diplomats, governors, judges, advisers and arbiters. The Wisdom literature of the ancient Near East is largely concerned with the training of such people, and its teaching is international. Thus, the biblical wisdom teaching in the book of Proverbs and elsewhere is presented to us as from King Solomon, the chief patron of Hebrew wisdom. King Hezekiah is also mentioned, and there are many references to court life. But there is little reference in the wisdom literature to Israel's distinctive faith and national history. Parts of the book of Proverbs are expressly presented as of foreign origin, being attributed to Agur son of Jakeh of Massa, and Lemuel, King of Massa.[14] Other parts of the book seem to come from Egypt. Interestingly, though, whereas in Egypt wisdom-teaching was aimed solely at high officials, in Israel it is to some extent democratized.[15] Arguably, something similar happened in India and China. The Buddha, Confucius and other teachers were at first much concerned with producing a class of cool and clear-headed counsellors and ministers to serve in public life. But as time went by the traditions were democratized. The calm and self-discipline of the civil servant were seen as qualities that other people too should emulate.

The civil servant or king's counsellor is someone who does not allow his or her own personal religious or moral convictions to obtrude. They are irrelevant. Indeed, if they were to become too salient they would diminish his usefulness. The task is to keep one's own personal convictions – if any – out of sight, and to give advice and service that is in the interests of the king and the state. You must be as rational and objective as you know how. And I am suggesting that there is a connection between the cool selfless-ness of the good political adviser, and the same quality as inculcated by the Buddha and others.[16]

We are talking about what I shall have to call 'therapeutic anti-moralism'. In religion and metaphysics many Westerners are inclined mistakenly to suppose that they will be better and happier if they believe more and believe it harder. But I have argued that in philosophy and religion the true way to salvation is by becoming more sceptical, anti-realist and beliefless. The more emptied-out inwardly you become, the more you are liberated from disabling anxiety and self-concern, and the more you are compelled to be creative in order to live. In ethics, the equivalent message will be that the trouble with so many of our fellow humans is not that they are not moral enough, but that they are so moral as to be moralistic. Their approvals and (especially) their disapprovals, their loves and (especially) their hates, their applause and (especially) their condemnations are all of them much too strong. Moralism blocks understanding and blocks compassion. The very last thing we should try to do is to instil even stronger moral principles into such people, for that would only have the effect of making them still more hostile and resentful than they are already. No, we should try to help most people to become morally less judgmental. Moralism makes people unhappy and deluded, and in any case is often quite irrelevant. Morality cannot be imposed upon people. It has to emerge as an authentic personal expression, and it needs a coolly friendly environment to help it to birth.

I cite a case that came my way recently. A few weeks before her marriage, a young woman discovered herself to have been made HIV-positive as a result of a rape suffered a few years earlier. Her ethnic background was such that if either her fiancé or her family were to learn about the rape or the HIV, she would immediately be cast out irrevocably. On the other hand she loved her fiancé and, knowing her life-expectancy now to be limited, longed for a child. The chance that she would transmit the HIV to her child was of the order of 22%. Condoms and low cunning gave her a fair chance of successfully avoiding transmitting the disorder to her husband. Should she then say nothing, allow the marriage to proceed, and hope for some years of happiness and a child? This strategy had after all, a better than even chance of success, at least in the short term, whereas the alternative – owning up – meant immediate and certain personal disaster. Either way, it was a fearsome choice to have to make alone.

This young woman presented herself to a counsellor, asking

for advice. The case shows, I suggest, the obnoxiousness and uselessness of moral realism, and of the lawcode metaphor for the nature of moral decision-making. The theory that in such a dilemma there is an objectively correct Answer, and that the professional's duty is merely to inform the client of it, is manifestly absurd. There is no sensible alternative to the modern counsellor's customary manner of dealing with such a case, which is to advise the client of current scientific knowledge that bears on the case and talk through the facts and the feelings involved, turning it over together and looking at it from different angles until the client finds herself coming to a decision of her own that she can live with. No other approach is humanly tolerable.

All of which is to say that moral realism has become morally repulsive, and we need to be cured of it. To be of any real moral use to the client, the counsellor has got to be morality-free. The counsellor has to be an ethical midwife who helps the client to produce a moral resolution of her own.

If that's how things are now, then what is the moral order in society, and in what way can we help to maintain it?

The problem is that when we encounter ethical subjectivism or emotivism, a very long literary tradition prompts us to fear disorder and anarchy:

> In those days there was no king in Israel;
>   every man did what was right in his own eyes.[17]

Monarchy in politics, theism in religion, foundationalism in philosophy and the patriarchal family have all been telling us for thousands of years that an objective authority is needed to define and maintain the moral order. Without such an authority, where are we?

The answer is not that we are reduced to pure individual egoism and self assertion, but that we fall back upon the slowly-evolving conversation of humanity, and upon the work of those politicians, writers, religious leaders and others who try to articulate such a consensus as will work here and now, and for the time being. In every area, there was never really anything else to fall back upon except a general consent. The procedures for conversing about the issue and for articulating the outcome of the debate may be more or less formalized. But in politics it has always been known that government requires the consent of the governed, and in religion the notion of consent as the criterion of truth goes back to antiquity, as is evidenced by the Vincentian canon, the *consensus fidelium*, the synod and the oecumenical council. So when we say in our neo-pragmatist manner that nowadays truth in every field is just a running conversation, a continuing argument, the state of the debate, then what we say is by no means entirely new. The difference is this: traditionally, truth was determined once by agreement, and thereafter held firm. It was possible subsequently to mythologize it as revealed truth, and forget the more human agreement in which it had begun. But today the parliament goes on forever. There is only ever small-t truth, the current state of the argument. Capital-T truth is never attained, because no really final vote ever gets to be taken. History goes on, making all truths lower-case. We cannot now mythologize our truths in quite the way we used to.

The moral order in society, on this account, is not a fixed entity. It is more like 'the culture', or 'the arts'. It is a living conversation, within which opposed views collide, criticisms are urged and fresh metaphors are introduced. Politicians have the delicate task of trying to arbitrate a consensus at just those points where the argument is fiercest. Often they will need to build into law the best consensus they can find. Hence the immense importance of their work, especially in those areas where the law is designed to give a moral lead. In our cooler and more generous moods we would judge capital punishment to be wrong, and hold that discrimination against people on the grounds of their sex or colour ought to be outlawed. So we encourage the politicians to legislate on the basis of our better selves, with the idea that the law thus enacted will function to protect us against our own worse selves. In this way, we use the law as an instrument of our own moral self-education, and give to the politicians the task of planning the development of the moral order.

Yet they, and it, are transient. Therapeutic anti-moralism implies that we recognize that the moral order is only a shifting human thing which is continuously being remade. Worse, it implies the paradox that we have a permanent duty to treat all moral values as ephemeral. We try to get around the paradox by claiming that values like freedom and justice don't change in themselves; only the manner in which we apprehend them changes. Unfortunately, this linguistic device invokes the old distinction between the thing in itself and the thing as apprehended by us. We are back to the contrast between reality and appearance – and we have seen that when philosophy goes linguistic that distinction collapses. We cannot make it work. In the present case, we have only our historically-conditioned ways of speaking about freedom and justice. We have no absolute and history-transcending vocabulary in which to define our values absolutely. We are only where we are, in a world in which everything is ephemeral and everything is open to criticism. Nothing is fixed or sacrosanct. Can we bear that; can we even so much as *say* it without paradoxicality? No wonder we humans have feared and dreaded transience so much. A world of pure transience or contingency certainly takes some getting used to.

Most actual democratic politicians are doubtless as flawed as everyone else, but we should greatly respect the politician as a type. She, he bears the brunt of transience. That is to say, we all find moral change acutely painful, and we relieve our pain by projecting it out as hostility and contempt against the politicians who have the job of managing moral change. Jewish legend has it that there are thirty-six hidden saints for whose sake God keeps the world in being. I suggest that most of them are politicians.

(v) Making good

We put the self up front, on our faces. That means we try to do without the traditional distinction between subjective selfhood and objective social relations, between psychology and sociology. On the contrary, my inmost subjectivity is vulnerable to and invaded by social goings-on. Conversely, my subjectivity lives and expresses itself in my social performances. I am the story of my life and the various roles I play.

It follows that we cannot really drop out. There is not any level at which the self is independent of the games it plays, the masks it wears and the battles it fights. The self is always involved in role-play and power-struggles. The traditional distinction between the religious life of monks and nuns and ordinary secular life in the world was a deception if it somehow led people to suppose that the monk was not acting a part in the human theatrical show, and not involved in questions of power. We are all involved – which means that Christian ethics cannot be represented as an ethic of authentic selfhood and powerlessness. What makes a life religious is the use to which power is put, rather than whether power is used at all.

The secular/religious distinction will therefore have to be re-expressed like this. Human life is organized into a very large number of game-situations or 'fields', as Bordieu calls them.[18] People get some kind of accreditation, licence, visa, qualification or training, which entitles them to operate in a field. They are cast in a role that entitles them to make various moves upon that field, and to engage in various sorts of symbolic exchange. Thus equipped and set moving, they struggle for various sorts of advantage. They seek moral, sexual or financial gain, they want status and recognition. Because (on my account of the self) every sentence I hear or read passes directly through my subjectivity, arousing my feelings and becoming apart of my selfhood, all language-use involves an exertion of power over others. In the media age, when the range of a voice can be so effectively extended by mechanical means, those who are highly articulate and have access to the media wield disproportionately great power. They can secure for themselves the lions' share of the available goods, both real and symbolic, and they do so.

The secular person, then, plays the various games for personal advantage. The religious person is as we have said an 'active non-realist', who refuses to accept existing rules and values as being sacrosanct. Instead, he or she criticizes and appraises existing games, valuations and symbols, and tries to change them. The aim is to revalue, to create value, and to optimize value. The religious person will seek to use power to make the inarticulate more vocal and the despised more valuable. So the religious person can be detected by the fact that she or he is always a little bit critical, a little bit subversive and rather unpopular. She plays the game all right, as everyone must. But she's not quite content simply to play it to her own advantage, as everyone else does. She'd like to find ways of playing the game that undermine it a little and have the effect of redistributing advantage towards the presently disadvantaged. So she's a bit ironical.

There is, however, no such thing as lasting success in this endeavour. We cannot expect ever to see a society which is perfect, decay-proof and conflict-free. All things are contingent and fleeting, and nothing ever quite gets to be wholly and securely complete and perfected. The point is most neatly shown in the way that linguistic meaning is delivered over time, but is never fully delivered. Time, which builds up, is always and ineluctably dismantling as well. That is what it is to be subject to temporal succession. The very coming-to-me of being and meaning is also, and identically, always their slipping-away-from-me.

Furthermore, nothing says that everybody must one day come into agreement. On the contrary, the human scene is always a power-struggle. Even the most fortunate and happily-married couple in the world are still scoring points off each other. In fact they must enjoy doing so, because conflict is sexy. All active human relationships have an element of conflict in them, because people have different interests and perspectives. Everybody must seek to define reality and posit values from her own angle.

Disagreement is inevitable and also interminable, because of the lack of any purely independent truth or value that might be invoked to settle the dispute. To see why this is so, consider the way in which there is no Real Truth about a marriage such as might be invoked to settle a dispute between the parties. That's what the human scene is like, and it's going to go on being like that. Complete harmony cannot be reached, because we have not the fully-independent basis upon which it might be reached. Cat and dog, management and workforce, politician and journalist, man and woman – we are at odds for ever. In fact, in popular culture we relish the theme of a perpetually feuding pair of complementary opposites, and find it abundantly illustrated in life. Every conversation is an argument. There's always a war of words, an element of rivalry, chemistry or sparks, a tussle for symbolic power and moral advantage. We cannot even imagine it otherwise, because the sparks are the sparks of life itself.

All these considerations bring the practical of the moral life very close to the practice of democratic politics. Is there a difference? Morality too is the art of the possible, an attempt to change things bit and to build the least bad moral order we can get for the moment. With such allies and friends as we can muster, we try to negotiate agreements, find and exploit loopholes, create new values, upgrade this and combat that. Denying system, we speak of 'issue ethics', on the analogy of issue politics. It is not the sort of work that is ever finished. Ethics has become an unending struggle for value, part of the political scene generally. Those on top can define reality, and may be expected to do so in their own interest. To challenge them you must get within range of them. This in turn means that you must engage with them in the games they play on their own ground. By definition, you will not be able to beat them in a straight fight, because they are the winners. They are on top. But you may be able to use laughter, cunning, deviousness or some other weapon.

On this last point, boo to Nietzsche. Of course we advocate a slave morality, or at least a slaves' moral policy. While the mighty are so firmly in their seats there is no way of budging them, except by borrowing some of the time-honoured stratagems of women, Jews, servants, satirists and other underdogs. No harm in that.

(vi)   The winged joy

To renew religious thought we must refocus it around the fleeting moment of language-formed experience, around the body and the senses. Religion will function as a therapeutic undoing of the dualisms posited by culture. For example, to make us conscious and to give us a psychological vocabulary, culture sets up body-mind dualism. This is done with great success, but with the side-effect that we become alienated from the life of the body. We need to relearn its sleepy complexity, its deep rhythms and its neglected sensory capacities. So the cultural movement that distinguished the mind from the body needs to be followed and counterbalanced by a therapeutic rediscovery of the body.

Now in a rather similar way the noun-verb distinction in the language certainly does a useful job in helping to establish an objective world of relatively-permanent objects, ordered in space and persisting through time. We think of these objects as moving around in conformity with mathematical laws of motion, interacting with each other and undergoing change. To explain change, we then split objects into two: there's an underlying substance that doesn't change, and it has 'accidental' properties or qualities that do change.

The effect of all this is to give us a rich world-picture, the world-picture of commonsense realism. It works pretty well for many everyday purposes. So far as the self is concerned, the effect is to make us two-levelled. For the purposes of morality, the civil law and (so we think) religion there needs to be a permanent self-identical self that does not change. It is the immortal and accountable soul, the subject of rights and duties, and it carries the can. We distinguish it from the ceaseless flux of our psychological states, our feelings and experiences, and the various ways in which we may grow and change over time.

All this makes it clear that the noun-verb distinction does a very good job. Empirically, it seems a fiction, for I cannot find a single bit of myself that has remained quite unchanged since my early youth. But for various legal and moral purposes I do need the notion of a persisting self which remains identically my mother's son, my wife's husband and so forth. So we posit such a self, and do so very successfully.

Unfortunately, there is a price to be paid. Substance cannot be reconciled with temporality, so the fictioning of the real self as an unchanging substance has the effect of alienating us from our own temporality, and therefore from life itself. Strangely and paradoxically, we need a therapeutic religious practice, not to get to heaven but in order to get back to our own life on earth. Salvation, the infinitely far-off and blessed goal of all religious striving, is nothing but a fully-achieved Yes to one's own temporality.

This is not easy. If, as I am suggesting, culture makes the world thinkable and negotiable by partly alienating us from our own temporality, and by leading us to look on everything as being a lot more stable than it is, the converse is that if we fully return into our own temporality the world will seem empty and void. There is a passage in one of the sutras where the Buddha speaks of time as flitting by tremendously fast. What does this mean? Compare the teaching of a Western phenomenalist who pictures the world as consisting of nothing but fleeting sense-data, snow-flakes hitting the window-pane of perception. From these atomic perceptions spread out over a flat screen the objective world is constructed by working outwards, and the self by working inwards. Fine – but not nearly sceptical enough, because each sense-datum is being pictured as itself a little mini-substance with a firm outline that endures for some moments. Really to do justice to the flux of time we will need a phenomenalism of phenomenalism, and so on forever, to get rid of the last residues of firm outlines and of substance. Which helps us, I suggest, to see why the Buddha pictures time as rushing by so fast that everything is a blur. Temporality or becoming a is a flux without either substance or structure.

If so, then, what are we trying to get back to and why? Isn't the attempt to throw off the cultural construction of the world, and return to the pure unstructured flux of temporal becoming, a futile enterprise? If it were to be successfully accomplished, it would surely leave us unable to say either that pure innocent becoming is 'blissful', or even that it is mere white noise. We could say nothing. So what on earth can be the point of a therapeutic philosophy or religious practice, if nothing can be said about what the cured state may consist in?

The answer I am suggesting is that what we are trying to regain is the temporality of language itself, as it moves over the deep, calling things into being and ordering the world. We are not trying to get out of language altogether. We are merely trying to get free from certain erroneous views about language. People tend to believe that there's a world out there whose structure language copies, they tend to suppose that the meaning of a word is the thing that it stands for, and they tend to forget that language is itself temporal. Language is not contemplative; it is, as we might say, committed to the active life. It is a worker, not a watcher. We escape from our errors when we grasp that language is an evolving social institution and a tool for the fulfilment of human purposes, that it really is temporal, that signification is itself flowing, differential and temporal, and that the world language so vividly evokes is only a human, projected world. It's not arbitrary: there are good reasons why it looks to us the way it does. But they are human reasons, reasons founded in us, our social organization and our requirements. So human life becomes outsideless, and the world a lot thinner than we had thought.

The consolation is that we are saved, healed, reunited with our own being-in-time. The winged joy, the non-clinging, non-acquisitive and *transient* happiness of those who can truly say yes to time. But there is no eternal life unless we give up the old illusory realism about both the world and the self. We have to lose our souls in order to gain them.

(vii) Being Time

Time is ubiquitous and all-pervasive, like God. Why is it so hard to get hold of? We might have expected there to be no problem. For example, I have suggested that the one-way successiveness of words in a sentence, and the continual production-and-passing-away of meaning as we scan along the lines, brings us as close to a direct apprehension of temporality as we can hope to get. The universal flowing successiveness of language-formed experience – that's *it*. Formation by language gives to the white noise of raw experience the ordered unidirectional successiveness that makes it truly temporal; and that is the sense in which time is our cultural creation. So language gives us temporality, and what more do we want?

Yet we remain dissatisfied. There is a hiatus between our existence and our temporality, between our being and the time of our lives. I have suggested that (amongst other things) it can be seen as a by-product of the noun-verb distinction. The sign-system that has given us consciousness has also alienated us, we fancy, from our original but lost immediacy. We cannot find our way back to that (perhaps mythical) state of immediacy, but we do find certain scars that seem to remind us of what we have lost. One of them is the awkwardness of the way the noun-verb distinction both sets up a world of permanent objects sitting about in space, and yet nevertheless assures us that everything flows. Language creates for us our necessary illusion – and then takes it away again. That is, language gives us what our science and technology need to have, namely a manageable, ordered, law-abiding world of stable objects and forces that we can manipulate. But by its movement, language undermines the tidy world that it seems to set up. We would rather like language to be a cool, neutral describer of a world independent of itself. Indeed, that is what many people actually suppose it to be. But unfortunately language is a creative and productive force. It shapes reality, it intervenes – and then it moves on.

There is then a certain conflict between substance and temporality, between the nominal aspect of language (the way it seems to conjure up and represent to us a stable ordered world of things) and the verbal aspect of language (its activity in time). Perhaps, then, we can fix things better by putting them down in writing? Speech is admittedly elusive. Almost before it has given to us, it is taking away again. But when something has been committed to writing, then it has surely been pinned down?

Unfortunately, similar paradoxes arise in relation to writing. True, writing is an attempt to oppose and resist the passage of time. But inevitably it is as temporal as anything else. It is produced in time, persists through time and is perused in time. If you are in time but trying to deny time, you become backward-looking. Writing is a solitary, substitute activity dependent upon memory and fantasy. It retires from the present and retreats into a dream of the past. And there is something deeply false about this. For language is a living, creative force that produces time, the world and the theatre of our social life; but the writer is trying to use the marker of time to stop the clock.

Writing is then both temporal and at odds with time. Certainly philosophy and theology have always found temporality difficult to represent or convey in writing. This, I suggest, is why the presentation of time in the classical texts about it is commonly mediated through a story, or a 'theatrical' situation in which the text fictions the question of time as arising. Most of the texts picture a solitary male thinker raising the question of time in some kind of interior monologue. But even within this general rubric there are considerable differences. One tradition, that of Augustine and the Christian monasticism influenced by him, raises the question of time in a context of prayer. The monk sits in his cell engaged in introspection. He examines himself and searches his memory before God, and he is a Christian platonist. So his thinking about time is governed by the contrast between the finite, temporal human subject and the infinite, eternal subject, God. God's unchangeable perfection shows up my changeableness and gives me the goal of my life – and now I see what time is. Time is the form of my creatureliness before God, who is my Beginning and my End.

In a second tradition another monk, Dōgen, thinks time while he is engaged in seated meditation for hours on end. He is 'just sitting', he tells us, 'thinking about nonthinking'. Like a naturalist in a forest, he has found that if you keep still enough for long enough all the birds and animals will come out for you. So Dōgen finds that as he meditates all things make themselves present to him, and that is beatitude. He experiences time as a self-renewing eternal Now in which he possesses all things.

Finally, there is a third tradition, that of the strenuous Protestant Soren Kierkegaard. In his text he pictures an individual much more involved in active life in the world. But he is still a solitary male, reflective and introverted. To stay upright and keep going, he must inwardly relate himself all the time to eternity by an ethical resolution of the will. Holding on to that, he can remain a true individual and steer a straight course through the oncoming flux of unpredictable and contingent events that is life in the world.

In mentioning these three different characters I am referring to three different literary persons: Augustine, in his *Confessions*, Book XI; Dōgen, in the *Uji* (being-time) fascicle of his *Shobogenzo*; and Kierkegaard's *Concluding Unscientific Postcript*. In each case the text recommends a spirituality by conjuring up what I have called a theatrical situation. We want to know what time is? – the text gives us a picture of an exemplary individual engaged in the practice of his religion, doing his own thinking in his own little theatre. He is a Western monk, a follower of Augustine sitting in his cell and searching his *memoria*, the depths of his own soul, before God. He is Dōgen, cross-legged in meditation and stock-still. He is Kierkegaard, the Protestant hero of faith, soldiering through life in this world. Each of these men is like a character in a play. He acts out his role, and it duly determines the way time appears to him. There isn't a True account of time; the way you experience the time of your life depends upon the way you choose to live. A treatise about time recommends a way of life.

What about us? Our time, I suggest, is the time of the emotions, of language and of our relationships. We take our idea of time not from sermons, prayer and philosophical texts, but from fiction, cinema and soap operas.

It is a big shift. Historically, Western reason tried to jump out of temporality. It wanted to stand still, it wanted to apply unchanging universal concepts, and it wanted to 'spatialize' the matter it was dealing with. Reason as we have known, or rather constituted, it so far has been a theological concept. It doesn't like the fact that because consciousness and language are inescapably successive, whatever we think of keeps slipping away from us even as we try to think it. Reason is happier with tenseless formal systems, and with the past, which looks relatively fixed, determinate and intelligible. Life in its movement is unmasterable by reason. Life comes at us, not necessitated, but contingent and largely unpredictable. Its logic, so far as it has one, is the temporally-extended or narrative logic of language and the emotions. We picture reason as being timeless and theological, but the root *mot* in words like emotion and motivated reminds us that our drives, passions and motives are discursive and temporally-extended in their form. This explains the literary tradition that views the heart as a better guide than reason to life in time. The heart and our feelings pulse in and with time and music and language.

If then the temporal biological life that we feel pulsing within us is indeed and outsidelessly the only life there can be for us, then we had better give up our confused dreams of a timefree and purely rational life. Reason must return into the movement of language, time and the passions, and spirit must return into flesh.

To grasp this, pause for a little experiment. Close your eyes and keep still for a moment. You feel that running train of thought as a train of words, or two or three distinct trains of words, running across your sensibility. It moves in precise harmony and concert with the motion of your own biological feelings. Indeed, the train of feelings represents itself to itself as a train of meanings. The cultural schooling you have had has made you into a perpetual-motion machine for generating language. All the time you are producing a rush of responses, simulations, object-hypotheses, theories and speculations. Words run back and forth non-stop, and their running to and fro is also and simultaneously the quivering of your own biological life. The movement in us of cultural meanings and the movement in us of biological feelings is one and the same movement, the movement of life itself, which is our being-time.

What more do you want? You are word-made-flesh, you are Christ, you are God incarnate. And this is outsidelessly all there is. So to be completely returned into the only truth of the human condition is liberation. Not release from the human condition, not deliverance from the world, but the return into the human condition, reconciled to it when we understand its outsidelessness.

(viii)   Now, outdate me!

The Greek word for a book is *biblos*, which is apt because every book by its very form aspires to the condition of a Bible. A long linear chain of signs that are perused over a period of some hours, it has a beginning, a middle and an end (as people say), and therefore incipiently a narrative form. In non-fiction books like this one, ideas play the roles of characters, but they are expected to behave consistently just as characters are. And in so far as a book is a well-made codex, it cannot help but take on the air of a codification. Furthermore, if it can interest a wide range of different readers then its story must be a universal story that operates at a range of different levels. So the book unifies its own diverse readership and range of applications. All of which means that every book, just by its form, looks as if it aims to be a rounded-off, biblical story-of-everything. In so far as it is finished and unified itself, it suggests that the world is so too.

But I have repudiated this. Our teaching has been anti-systematic. We quoted Kierkegaard as saying, against Hegel, that the way our life keeps moving on prevents us from ever getting it satisfactorily fixed in a system. We haven't got, says Kierkegaard, a still point from which to observe life. We are characters held within the movement of the story (I think he may mean) who can't jump out and review the narrative as a whole. But it is worse than that, because since Kierkegaard's time we have become aware of the way even ostensibly non-historical systems of thought can suddenly become historically obsolete. Aristotelean formal logic, Euclidean geometry, Newtonian physics: everything dates.

So what about this present book? It is still possible, I suggest, to be anti-realist and anti-systematic, and yet to represent your teaching in reasonably clear form – perhaps even with short summaries – provided you also include the right sort of warnings on the packet. Consider the case of Buddhist teaching, which was commonly presented in very clear style all the way through from the early Madhyamika to Zen. In an important sense these great movements were anti-systematic. But they made much use of the traditional Buddhist mnemonic formulae, at least as teaching devices. I think I'll have to say something similar. This book is a false system. See it as just a mnemonic to get you started. Don't make a fetish of it. Think of Dorothy Parker, reviewing the book and saying: 'This is not a book to be lightly tossed aside. It should be thrown, with force.' Similarly, leave this book behind. Forget it. Since out there there is no true and unchanging Truth, there is no true doctrine and no crisp epitome of the Truth. This book is related to my other books as one painting is related to other paintings by the same artist. I circle obsessively around certain themes, reworking them, looking for interesting new angles and insights – but finality, No. Dogmatic truth, No. So move on now. Make believe. Make, believe. Fare well.

Notes

Preface

1. Cited in Joan Stambaugh, *Impermanence is Buddha-Nature: Dōgen's Understanding of Temporality*, Honolulu: U. of Hawaii 1990, p.27. Dōgen (1200–1253) founded the Sōtō Zen school in Japanese Buddhism. The best book about him so far, by general consent, is Carl Bielefeldt, *Dōgen's Manuals of Zen Meditation*, Berkeley: University of California 1988.
2. Short account in Shlomo Biderman, 'Scepticism and Religion: On the Interpretation of Nagarjuna'; in Roy W. Perrett (ed.), *Indian Philosophy of Religion*, Dordrecht: Kluwer 1989, pp.61–74.
3. Umberto Eco, *Art and Beauty in the Middle Ages*, Yale University Press 1986.
4. My friend Michael Goulder draws this conclusion in Goulder and John Hick, *Why Believe in God?*, SCM Press 1983, ch.1.
5. For the title of this book, see the quotations from Dōgen's treatise on *Uji*, being-time, in Stambaugh, cited above, especially pp.24, 36.

1 Redefinitions

1. A good essay on all this is Arthur Danto's 'Approaching the End of Art', printed in his collection *The State of the Art*, Prentice Hall 1987, and reprinted in Peter Abbs (ed.), *The Symbolic Order*, Lewes, Sussex: The Falmer Press 1989, ch.11. But Danto's interpretations are very different from mine. A bit more congenial is B.R. Tilghman, *But is it Art?*, Oxford: Blackwell 1984.
2. The ever-admirable Richard Rorty has a short and recent piece on this in his Introduction to John P. Murphy, *Pragmatism: From Pierce to Davidson*, Boulder: Westview Press 1990. The piece is entitled 'Pragmatism as Anti-Representationalism'.
3. For the veiled sexism of the appearance-reality distinction, see the long

and eloquent denunciation of women by Jake at the end of Kingsley Amis's novel *Jake's Thing* (1978). It is highly instructive for the way it imputes to women all the traditional characteristics of the world of appearance – vapidity, fickleness, shallowness, and undue concern with images and outward show.

4. See George Pattison, *Art, Modernity and Faith*, Macmillan 1991, especially ch.4.
5. Text from the Aldine Press edition.
6. For the following discussion, see Matsuo Bashō, *The Narrow Road to the Deep North, and other Travel Sketches* translated by Nobuyuki Yuasa, Harmondsworth: Pelican Classics 1966.
7. Bashō, op.cit., p.37.
8. On these ideas see my *The Long-Legged Fly*, SCM Press 1987.
9. I should say that I am by no means the first to suggest the relevance to us of figures such as Bashō. The Imagist movement, almost a century ago, was strongly influenced by Japanese poetry.

2 *Parts, not Souls*

1. II Corinthians 4.16.
2. Charles Taylor, *Sources of the Self*, Cambridge 1989.

3 *The Six Truths*

1. *Republic*, vii. 514A-521B.
2. Compare St Paul: 'Now we see only puzzling reflections in a mirror, but then we shall see face to face.' (1 Corinthians 13.12).
3. Hilary Putnam, *Meaning with a Human Face*, Harvard 1990.
4. Hence the concept of 'anti-realism', invented by Nietzsche. It is not so much a doctrine in its own right, as a polemic and a cure for the sickness caused by Plato.
5. Peter Goodrich, *Languages of Law*, Weidenfeld 1990. The puzzle is that so many of our special vocabularies, such as those of morality, religion and law, seem to get away with claiming a lot more authority and objectivity than they are entitled to. How do they do it?
6. Umberto Eco, *Semiotics and the Philosophy of Language*, Macmillan 1984.
7. A phrase used by Ernst Troeltsch and other historians of his generation. The idea has been traced back as far as Vico.
8. How, as Zarathustra puts it, can 'the chaos within' become 'a dancing star'? Leslie Paul Thiele, in his *Friedrich Nietzsche and the Politics of*

the Soul, Princeton 1990, interprets the philosopher as striving to forge an heroic individual selfhood out of disparate and warring materials. But Nietzsche sees the self as laboriously forming itself out of pre-existing biological constituents, whereas on my account all the self's parts are not just formed, but even produced, by culture. There is no quite independent substrate to work on. The self is exposed to cultural winds that blow right through it, and is not going to become more integrated than the culture that has produced it. Ethically, its best course is to pour itself back into, and try to contribute something to, the public realm. So whereas Nietzsche and Foucault teach a pagan ethic of stylish self-mastery and self-perfection, I teach a Christian ethic of self-realization, to be gained only through self-emptying, self-giving, self-loss. Selfhood is expression, going out into communication.

4 Life Time

1. Good tribute in Stephen Houlgate, *Hegel, Nietzsche and the criticism of metaphysics*, Cambridge 1986.
2. For the emergence of this idea within the orthodox analytical tradition, see Bernard Williams, *Moral Luck*, Cambridge 1981, no.5, 'Conflicts of values'.
3. Matthew Tindal's book title, *Christianity as old as the Creation* 1730, plays (no doubt mischievously) upon our will to reify and to retroject.
4. On Buddhist non-realism, see Francis H. Cook, 'Zen and the Problems of Language'; in Joseph Runzo, *Realism and Non-Realism in Religion*, Macmillan (forthcoming).

5. The World of Signs

1. The subject of animal communication is at least broached in J.M. Cullen, 'Some Principles of Animal Communication'; in R.A. Hinde (ed.), *Non-Verbal Communication*, Cambridge 1972.
2. Claude Lévi-Strauss, *The Savage Mind*, Weidenfeld and Nicholson 1966, ch.5; *Totemism*, Penguin Books 1969, Introduction by Roger Poole, pp.59–63.
3. There is interesting material on obsessive pattern-hunting in Jean-Jacques Lecercle, *Philosophy through the Looking-Glass*, Macmillan 1985: especially on Saussure, pp.2–6.
4. See Michel Foucault's classical discussion in *The Order of Things*, 1966 (ET Tavistock Publications 1970), ch.2.

5. See my *The Long-Legged Fly*, SCM Press 1987, and *Creation Out of Nothing*, SCM Press and Trinity Press International 1990.

6. Terry Eagleton uses the word in *The Ideology of the Aesthetic*, Blackwell 1990; but who used it before he did?

7. As David Hume already says so well: *Dialogues Concerning Natural Religion*, 1779, Dial.IV.

8. P.W. Atkins, *The Creation*, W.H. Freeman 1981; Richard Dawkins, *The Selfish Gene*, Granada Publishing 1979; *The Blind Watchmaker*, Longman 1986.

9. Mircea Eliade, *The Myth of the Eternal Return*, Routledge 1954, ch.1.

10. Exceptions? On a reasonably generous account of their thinking: Hobbes, Spinoza, perhaps Hume. Recently: Nietzsche, Ryle, Merleau-Ponty. Try David Michael Levin, *The Body's Recollection of Being*, Routledge 1985.

11. As Foucault acknowledges (*The Care of the Self*, Random House 1986), 'puritanism' about sex is much older than Christianity. The best account of classical Christian attitudes is by general consent Peter Brown, *The Body and Society*, Faber 1988.

12. My thinking of these matters was much helped by Henry Staten, *Wittgenstein and Derrida*, Blackwell 1985. See the discussion of Augustine on pp.136–139.

13. Ray Bradbury, *The Illustrated Man*, Hart Davis 1952. Who invented the term 'body-language'?

14. The term 'situations' is used by language-teachers who get children to play the parts of customer and shopkeeper, diner and waiter, and so on.

15. See at least the opening chapters of Douglas Kellner, *Jean Baudrillard*, Polity Press 1989. Baudrillard's books are very unsound indeed, but he does open up the territory.

16. Eco has compared our modern world of images with that of the Middle Ages; but it has I think not been said before that late capitalism is still theological in the synthesis of predestined order, personal freedom, duty and desire that it seeks to achieve.

17. See my 'The Last Judgement'; in *Predictions: Darwin Lectures, 1991* (forthcoming).

6 *What is Wrong with us*

1. Kingsley Amis, in his *Memoirs*, emphasizes that Larkin was terrified not merely of dying, but even more of the state of being dead.

2. See S.G.F. Brandon, *The Judgment of the Dead*, Weidenfeld and Nicholson 1967; and John Hick, *Death and Eternal Life*, Macmillan

1976. Unfortunately these surveys, like others, appear to make the error of supposing that when you have examined the teachings of all the faiths and philosophies, you have somewhere before you at least the makings of the correct answer to your question. No, you haven't. The correct answer in religion, as in philosophy and in art, is that you must first become as steeped in the whole tradition as the best professionals, and then you must invent something quite new out of your own head. First total immersion, and then pure invention. There is no other path. If you practise only scholarship, you're dead. If you practise only pure invention, you're a nut. You must do both, because as the teachers say, truth is as old as the hills and has to be reinvented every morning.

3. Paul Tillich, *The Courage to Be*, Nisbet 1952; *Systematic Theology* Volume 1, Nisbet 1953; Bernard Martin, *Paul Tillich's Doctrine of Man*, Nisbet 1966.

4. E.g. Mary Douglas, *Purity and Danger*, Routledge 1966; *Natural Symbols*, Barrie and Rockliff 1970.

5. I acknowledge a debt here to Donald Davidson's recent writings about language. Summary of his ideas in Bjorn Ramberg, *Donald Davidson's Philosophy of Language*, Blackwell 1989.

6. Compare my discussion with Ninian Smart, *The Philosophy of Religion*, Sheldon Press 1979, and the very interesting David Wood, *Philosophy at the Limit*, Unwin Hyman 1990, esp. ch.1.

7. Mircea Eliade, *The Myth of the Eternal Return* (previously cited ch.5 n.9).

8. In fact, though, much of what is said in this section may be found in Hegel's *Phenomenology of Spirit*.

9. The contrast between our discursive understanding and God's intuitive understanding was still important to Kant: *Critique of Judgment*, §77.

10. Nietzsche saw this. Our consciousness and our vision of the world are produced by and within language – which is and cannot help but be a bunch of well-worn tabloid clichés. To break out of those clichés we must coin new metaphors, use our imaginations and *innovate*. See *The Gay Science*, §354, etc.

11. E.g. *The Concept of Anxiety*, Princeton edition XII, 1980, pp.64ff, 92ff.

12. Michael Argyle and Benjamin Beit-Hallahmi, *The Social Psychology of Religion*, second edition, Routledge 1975, p.70. See also G.E.W. Scobie, *The Psychology of Religion*, Batsford 1975, pp.55f., 159f.

13. Reprinted in Vol.V of the *Collected Papers*, ed. Charles Hartshorne and Paul Weiss, Harvard 1931–4, and in the *Selected Writings* edited by Philip P. Weiner under the title *Values in a Universe of Chance*,

New York: Doubleday Anchor 1958. See also W.B. Gallie, *Pierce and Pragmatism*, Penguin 1952, ch. 3; and – very brief and clear – John P. Murphy, *Pragmatism*, Boulder Colorado: Westview Press 1990, ch. 1. Pierce, on Murphy's view, is particularly far-sighted in his denial that we can know intuitively that some idea is purely original and founding, and not determined by any other. We cannot be sure that we have got back to the very beginning.

14. In the 'Faculties' paper, under Question Two. See Wiener, op. cit., p.28.

15. For Nietzsche on consciousness, see Arthur Danto, *Nietzsche as Philosopher*, Columbia 1965, pp.116–122; Leslie Paul Thiele, *Friedrich Nietzsche and the Politics of the Soul*, Princeton 1990, esp. pp.91–95.

16. Gilbert Ryle, *The Concept of Mind*, Hutchinson 1949; Ludwig Wittgenstein, *Philosophical Investigations*, Blackwell 1953.

17. For really beautiful denials of 'intuitive self-consciousness' and 'privileged access', see Pierce in Wiener, pp.25–30, and Ryle, pp.167–181.

18. The chief text is Derrida's introduction to Husserl's *The Origin of Geometry*, 1962; trans. J. Leavey, Brighton: Harvester 1978. Notice that the way Derrida questions the appeal to founding intuitions resembles the way Pierce did so, in a very different cultural setting.

19. Ryle, pp.11f.

20. C.W. Huntington, Jr, *The Emptiness of Emptiness: an Introduction to Early Indian Mādhyamika*, Hawaii 1989. Part One of this book contains one of the most useful essays yet published on the affinities between the Madhyamika and modern Western philosophy as practised by Wittgenstein and Derrida.

21. See Joan Stambaugh, op.cit. (Preface, n.1).

22. J.M.E. McTaggart, 'The Unreality of Time'; *Mind* 18, pp.457–474 (1908); *The Nature of Existence* Volume II, ed. C.D. Broad, Cambridge 1927; D.H. Mellor, *Real Time*, Cambridge 1981.

7   *The cure*

1. Paul Tillich, *Systematic Theology*, Vol.I, Nisbet 1953, ch. VII, pp.181–206.

2. *Journals* 1 A 130; the early Kierkegaard's treatment of the classical-romantic distinction is a little like Nietzsche on the Apollonian and the Dionysiac. G. Malantschuk, *Kierkegaard's Thought*, Princeton 1974, pp.48ff.

3. David Wood, *Philosophy at the Limit*, Unwin Hyman 1990, p.18.

4. Charles Segal, *Lucretius on Death and Anxiety: Poetry and philosophy in 'De Rerum Natura'*, Princeton 1990.
5. *Critique of Pure Reason*, A615 = B643, etc. Kant's critique of the errors of objectifying thought begins to bring the West closer to the East.
6. Cited in C.W. Huntington Jr (see ch.6, n.20 above), pp.141ff.
7. Yūhō Yakoi, *Zen Master Dōgen: An Introduction with Selected Writings*, New York: Weatherhill 1976, pp.39ff.
8. *Mūlamadhyamikakārikā*, 19f., cited in Joan Stambaugh (see Preface, n.1), p.5.
9. Stambaugh, p.62.
10. *A Treatise of Human Nature*, Book I, Part IV, Sect. VI.
11. Jean Piaget and Bärbel Inhelder, *The Psychology of the Child*, Routledge 1969, pp.14f. Somewhat to my surprise, Piaget, even in this last summary of his ideas, still puts the 'object concept' earlier than 'object relations' (i.e., the permanent thing before the other person). He still places the cognitive act of recognizing a permanent thing out there before his account of the transference of libido from narcissism on to the mother. In my text I have nevertheless put the mother first.
12. 'The universe of the young baby is a world without objects, consisting only of shifting and unsubstantial "tableaux".' Ibid.
13. See *Twilight of the Idols*, 'Maxims and Arrows', 16, 27; and 'How the "Real World" at last became a Myth'; and Jacques Derrida, Spurs/Eperons, Chicago 1979, pp.83ff.
14. Cited in Lynn A. de Silva, *The Problem of the Self in Buddhism and Christianity*, Macmillan 1979, p.69; and see ch.7 as a whole for a typical discussion of nirvana.
15. Plato invented the concept of mental health: Anthony Kenny, *The Anatomy of the Soul*, Blackwell 1973. Since the Second World War various radicals, including Thomas Szasz and Michael Foucault, have been trying to get rid of it. With good reason, in so far as norms of health, sanity and so on are set up in order to justify depriving certain people of their liberties.

8 How we should live

1. Nietzsche revived the notion that self = *persona* = mask. There is also some good philosophy of theatre in Lyotard. Otherwise, we seem to be very short of philosophical reflection around the thesis that there is no way to selfhood except through the way you play a role. This is very odd, if we pause to consider that nowadays the chief available

models of successfully expressed selfhood are various types of player, performer and interpreter.

2. Mark 2. 27f. Questions of historical criticism etc. are quite irrelevant to these remarks.

3. Matthew 6. 34.

4. Luke 17. 21 (here, however, the question of the best translation of *entos* cannot be ignored).

5. Matthew 5. 39.

6. E.g., Jean-Christopher Agnew, *Worlds Apart: The Market and the Theatre in Anglo-American Thought*, 1550–1750, Cambridge 1900.

7. J.A. Barish, *The Antitheatrical Prejudice*, Berkeley: University of California 1981.

8. Michael Goldman, *Acting and Action in Shakespearean Tragedy*, Princeton 1985.

9. S. Kierkegaard, *The Anxieties of the Heathen* (1848), and *The Lilies of the Field and the Birds of the Air* (1849); in *Christian Discourses*, trs. Walter Lowrie, New York: Oxford University Press 1940.

10. See the good discussion in Alistair Hannay, *Kierkegaard*, Routledge 1982, pp.139–146, from which source also I have borrowed the quotations from the *Postscript*, etc.

11. So I disagree with George Pattison, 'From Kierkegarrd to Cupitt: Subjectivity, the Body and Eternal Life'; *Heythrop Journal* XXXI (1990) pp.295–308, who argues that I have moved a very long way from SK.

12. No doubt this can never be asserted without a certain reflexive paradoxicality. And indeed, those who know me best regard me as an opinionated old sod. But we can live with the difficulty, and try to reduce our own inconsistency.

13. On all this, see my 'Unsystematic Ethics and Politics', in Philippa Berry and Andrew Wernick, *Shadow of Spirit* (forthcoming).

14. Proverbs 30.1; 31.1.

15. See J.C. Rylaarsdam's discussion, in Matthew Black and H.H. Rowley, (ed.) *Peake's Commentary on the Bible*, Nelson 1962, p. 444.

16. Trevor Ling, *The Buddha*, London: Temple Smith 1973.

17. Judges 17.6; 21.25; and see also Deuteronomy 12.8.

18. Pierre Bordieu, *Outline of a Theory of Practice*, Cambridge 1977; *Language and Symbolic Power*, Cambridge: Polity Press 1989. And see Richard Harker, Cheleen Mahar and Chris Wilkes (ed.), *An Introduction to the Work of Pierre Bordieu*, Macmillan 1990.

INDEX OF NAMES